DIRT FROM OUR EARS,

MUD FROM OUR EYES

RETROSPECTIONS OF A
WHITE ABORIGINAL ELDER

By

Robert McKeich PhD

Published by RobiGayle LLC

www.robertmckeich.com

McKeich, Robert, PhD

Dirt from our ears, mud from our eyes
Retrospections of a white Aboriginal elder

2011

ISBN 978-1463602550 (pbk.)

Library of Congress Control Number: 2011932304

*Aboriginal photos sourced from the Robert McKeich collection
of the State Library of Western Australia and reproduced with
the permission of the Library Board of Western Australia.*

Contents

PREFACE

These stories are dedicated to my great grandson, Aubrey Robert Sweet, born in Melbourne on January 12, 2011, and to my four children, 11 grandchildren, and fourteen great grandchildren.

I chose Aubrey Robert for two reasons. He is the latest of my line to be born, and I shall never meet him before I make my final journey in this world. Also, because I am honored that he carries my name, Robert. It is likely that when he grows up he may wish to know something about his great grandfather. My own great grandfather, Robert McKeich, had the distinction of being the last man killed in the Boer, South African War (1899-1902). A dubious honor to be sure, but there is a kind of mystique associated with that.

I believe that my life has more significance than my death, so I have chosen several samples of adventurous experiences that molded and changed me. Here are glimpses into my childhood, my marriages, Aboriginal wisdom, religious and existential thoughts, teaching, travel, and a visit with my fantasy and poetic world. Directly and indirectly there are 'messages' to be found in the allegory of the milkman, the whimsy of the rabbit and the teacher, the potential depth of existentialism, the emergence of life truths through the death of an Aboriginal elder, and thoughts on the meaning of marriage.

There is much more I could have shared and you may find it in the Battye Library Archives in Perth, and with your Granddad Paul in Mount Barker. I never missed a day in writing my Journals since 1978. Poems, emails, photos, and correspondence supplement these adventures and thoughts.

I took life seriously but not so seriously that I could not enjoy it, or even more importantly, that I was able to laugh at myself. To maintain my integrity and peace of mind, I developed a set of guiding principles that have sustained me, whether times were 'good' or 'bad', recognizing that good and bad were what I made of the circumstances. *Respect, Responsibility, Commitment*, and *Creativity* were, and still are, my themes. I also took chances.

In 1954, at 30 years of age, with my wife Betty, and children John 10, Miriam 9, Paul 4, and Julie Ann 2 we left Auckland, New Zealand for Cundeelee, a remote mission settlement in the Western Australian desert, to pioneer the first government school, and to evangelize the Aborigines. Over time, I changed my religious, dogmatic demands, and identified so closely with the Aborigines that 21 years later I was eventually initiated into the *Wangkayi* tribe by the Cundeelee community with a painful ceremony.

I pursued studies to the PhD level; travelled to exotic places to observe and meet the people; moved from one marriage to another; satisfied my curiosity, and developed a wider world view, greater tolerance for differences, plus a more compassionate and peaceful life. I reviewed my fundamentalist conservative religious position in the Baptist church, and my evangelical pursuits that had tied me in to a dependency mode. By withdrawing my interests in the church expectations I liberated my behavior, which allowed me to take responsibility for my choices.

I express my sincere thanks to many people who have contributed to my life. My parents raised me during the difficult years of the Great Depression and gave me the opportunities for my early education. My teachers, and the students who also were my teachers, and my colleagues, enlightened and challenged me. With Betty, my first wife, and our four children John, Miriam, Paul and Julie Ann, who shared some of the adventures recorded in this book, I learned that my family was a unit worth treasuring. The Aborigines of Cundeelee contributed immeasurably to my awareness of the wider world and my growth within it. My gradual understanding of their ways, and the devastating impact of European culture on theirs, plus their example of being tuned in with Nature, transformed my entire life.

Special thanks are warranted for my wife Gayle whose companionship over many years has delighted my being. We shared some of the adventures recorded in Dirt from our Ears, Mud from our Eyes, and worked together on this book project. Together we have travelled the world, camping and bicycling, following trails and creating our own, eventually in ecstasy laughing with joy.

Then there is Christo Norden-Powers (www. thepracticeofstillness.com) who emerged back into my life after almost 30 years apart, urging me to write my story, and then sharing the editing and production. His partner Edwina Van Der Westhuizen (www.spandah.com) graciously prepared the work for publication. Finally there is Vickie Lea Anderson whose sparkling personality spurred me on when health concerns seemed overwhelming.

Chapter One

REMINISCENCES OF A MILKMAN

If my destiny should be consignment to hell, I know what punishment has been prepared for me by the devil, or is it God? I'm never quite sure. I shall be delivering milk throughout the eternal night. Not that this would be related in any way to any particular sin, but because it was the one job I grew to dislike more than any other.

I'm taking you back to 1947. I remember it well. I had been recently discharged from serving three years in the New Zealand armed services, had two children and another on the way, and was very short on money. I decided to supplement my meager teacher's income of less than $100.00 month by doing a little night work. I became a licensed taxi driver, but there were no openings for night drivers. A friend - I called him that then, but now I am not so sure - introduced me to this new lifestyle. I needed the money. The hours seemed to fit around my teaching commitments. It was a healthy occupation, out in the open air, plenty of exercise, no great mental demands, and the money was reasonable. Not a lot, but reasonable.

So I started. It did not take long to establish a routine. Out of bed at 11 p.m., a ride of seven miles on my bicycle to the milk factory, feed Horse, load the wagon, hitch up Horse,

1

drive out onto the road not before 1.30 a.m. by law, but earlier if you could get away with it, deliver milk until about 7.30 a.m., back to the factory, park the wagon, unhitch Horse, put him in the stable and feed him, check in at the office, and finally on the bicycle for the seven-mile ride home. Shower, breakfast, and cycle to school three miles away. Teach all day. Home by 4.30 p.m., time with the kids, chores, dinner, and to bed maybe by 7.30 p.m. School five days a week, but milk deliveries every day without a break. Not easy. My children were too young to remember. They were not aware of what their parents must choose to do to provide. Kids can afford to take life for granted.

Getting up after only a few hours sleep is bad enough, but what if you can't sleep? Naturally noisy children, a worried mind, overtiredness, and an aching body unused to such physical activities - all of these undermined any attempt to relax. There would be no chance of catching up until the next night. Get up, no matter what the weather, no matter how you felt, and dress in the darkness so as not to wake the wife and kids. Don't bother with a cuppa; no time, and it may disturb someone. Creep out into the darkness.

Cycling was OK on fine nights when there was little wind, but on wet or windy nights, especially in midwinter, the trip was tough and dangerous. Careless motorists introduced a danger that pursued me throughout the night. Weekends were the worst, in the early hours, after parties. Occasionally the 'near misses' were scary.

Horse, seemingly so docile and friendly, patiently stood in his stall. But horses can sometimes be as deceptive as people. Feed him. Now load the large four wheel wagon with wire crates of glass bottles, including quarts, pints, half pints, and two 20 gallon cans of 'loose' milk. Check the lights again on the milk cart to make sure the battery was charged. If not, there was nothing to be done about it now. I then lead Horse out and back him into the shafts. Ready to go?

2

Not quite. Before mounting the wagon, I had to make sure that the brakes were really tightly applied, or I was certainly in for trouble, or at least more trouble than what usually followed. Horse had been mistreated by the former milko who habitually jumped on the wagon and immediately poked poor old Horse in the backside to get him moving. With such conditioning, Horse was like a tightly coiled spring. Now, as soon as he felt the touch of a foot on the step, he would take off at speed, not daunted by the heavy load, or the fully applied brakes. Imagine the nightly drama of Horse and his wagon careering headlong down the wide driveway, gathering speed rapidly, sparks flying from the rear wheels, and then racing out across a busy four lane road, to make a sharp right, almost overturning on the way. In the one-and-a-half years we played this early version of chicken, it was only the kindness of God who saved us, timing the run so that the motor traffic was somewhere else.

The maliciousness of night-time deliveries was compounded by the street lights going out at 1.30 a.m. It was difficult to see where to deliver the milk, and it was quite dangerous with a dark wagon on the darkened streets, especially if the one small taillight was being fed from an almost dead battery. Several careless motorists almost came to grief with their last earthly view being the rear end of my milk wagon. I carried a flashlight on my belt alongside the money satchel. This was necessary in order to see my way up the alleys, between the walls of buildings, up the stairways of tall apartments, behind hedges, and around obstacles. Of course it was also indispensable for reading The Book. The worst nights were the moonless, overcast, or rainy ones, and New Zealand was notorious for its rainfall.

The Book. Experienced milkos do not need The Book. For those starting out on a run The Book was essential, but it could also be a trap. Clear memories of my first three nights of introduction to the route remain to haunt me forever. So do the fourth, fifth, sixth, and more. All because of The

Book.

On my first night I was introduced to the system of distribution by the milko whose run I was taking over. With 300 gallons to deliver, in small quantities, to about 700 customers, including shops and delicatessens, I was a most confused new chum as dawn broke at the completion of my first round. That first night I had been sent on random small deliveries to 'acclimatize' myself to the work.

Night two was better organized, or so it seemed. My teacher took one side of each street, and I took the other.

"Get 3, 4, 2, and the loose, and deliver 1, 3, 2 loose, 1½, 2½, 3, and 2 loose up there, #65 behind the hedge, #67 on the verandah, #69 in the mailbox, miss one, the rest in mail boxes by the gates."

Translated that meant:

"Put 3 quart bottles, 4 pint bottles, and 2 half pints in your wire carrying basket, and take the four-gallon can of loose milk". You've probably guessed that house number 65 needs one pint behind the hedge, and don't forget to collect the empties, 67 wants 3 pints (one quart and one pint bottle) on the verandah, and so on. What could be simpler? This job was a pushover. However, after repeating different combinations of the formula for at least six hours, my mind was boggling. Night three repeated the same routines except that the teacher took my side tonight, and I took his.

I haven't forgotten The Book. All of these delivery formulae were recorded there, along with the names, addresses, variations over the weekend, and comments such as the reliability of customers to pay their bills, "watch for dog," and so on.

On the fourth night, on my own, with my companion Horse, and armed with these secret codes, I sallied forth. After loading the wagon, hitching Horse, remembering to apply the brakes, and successfully negotiating the dramatic exit on to the main road, I was singing with confidence at 1.15 a.m. on a bright moonlit morning. All went well at first, reinforcing my apparent success with such an easy job. This I could master in no time. I then began to grow uneasy. I was getting clues that all was not going according to schedule. Fairly consistently I was collecting the wrong number and size of empties, sometimes there were no billycans for the loose milk, I could not find the delivery spot, this house looked empty, and I vaguely remembered that we used a different order in running the streets. Then it dawned on me. The Book, now my sole guide to deposit 300 gallons of milk in 700 separate locations, was not correct. It had not been brought up to date.

All the tensions, anxieties, frustrations, fears, alienations, angers, and so on, about which psychologists so expertly write, became part of my stress syndrome. I felt like crying, but laughed when I thought it was no use crying over undelivered milk. There was no way to remember the training of the previous three nights, so I followed The Book. Perhaps there was a religious message in there somewhere, but I was not in the mood to look for one, except to plead God's help and forgiveness for the wrongs I was committing, the sins of frustration and impolite thoughts, and to ask for protection from the wrath of the customers. I was no longer singing with confidence.

The next night I received more notes and letters than a successful pop idol. At least they helped me to sort out some of the mess in The Book. By the end of the second week things were about right. In addition, I was beginning to travel the route from memory, without the need to refer to my guiding myth.

Delivering milk was tough. Not only were the hours wrong for my body rhythms, especially with the teaching commitment as well, but I must have walked and run about ten miles each night, as well as riding the fourteen miles on my bicycle. The loads were heavy, taking their toll on my back and legs, which to this day are affected by the strain. Some men of a different physique managed fine, but my current arthritis and spinal surgery can be traced to my nights on the milk run. However, at that time I needed the money to provide for my small family, and I thought the costs were worth the pain and discipline.

Fortunately Horse knew the run better than I, so he was a great help - most of the time. He followed or preceded me up the road, and waited at the next delivery spot. He almost always came when I whistled, and he never complained about the weather, at least not to me (but who knows what was said back at the stables). However, there was one time, at 7 a.m., with the beginning of the early morning commuter rush, when he decided to make a sudden U turn on a major highway, and spilled several crates of empties right across the road. I did not know whether to stay and clean up the broken glass, or to chase the fast disappearing horse and wagon down the road. Fortunately a kindly customer, collecting his milk and morning paper, or maybe scooping up Horse's droppings for his garden, volunteered to sweep up the dangerous mess, while I hiked a mile to rescue my transportation.

'Notes' were part of the job. We lived in two cultures, the customers and I, with our communication being solely in the medium of notes from them and milk from me. They certainly didn't want to join my culture, but they did not know how I longed to share theirs. Many a night I could have dropped into bed, any bed, or none at all, so long as I could get some sleep. One night I received a note from a customer, which read,

"Dear Milko, I do not mind your horse eating my hedge, but I do object to the heavy thump and rattle of bottles at 3 a.m. when the cart wheels hit the curbing."

I showed it to Horse, and he stopped eating the hedge.

Another note, obviously from an intellectual, well-educated customer, one morning read,

"This day I require a zero quantity of lactic secretion from the mammary glands of the female of the bovine species."

6

There were a few lighter moments.

Most of the milk we delivered was pasteurized, bottled and sealed under hygienically inspected conditions. We also carried the loose milk. I never found out whether it was pasteurized or not, although I suspected it was from the same vats as that in the bottles. However, if the customer wanted it pasteurized, then that is how it was. If he wanted it 'raw' then that is how it was, all out of the same can. Some preferred loose milk for their own reasons. They claimed it 'tasted better', 'the bottles were not clean,' 'it contained more cream,' 'it was a different color,' or whatever they thought best. If they only knew. The loose milk came in large 20 gallon cans which, if not stirred properly before transfer to the smaller 4 gallon delivery container, could give more or less cream. Milk was not homogenized in those days.

I handled the harness, stroked and caressed Horse, opened dirty gates, put my fingers into unwashed empties, patted territorial dogs, and in general managed to maintain unhygienic hands. When the pint dipper fell into the bottom of the delivery can, it was retrieved by the manual method, to the obvious pollution of the milk. On occasions, when I threw up the lid to make a delivery, a shower of hedge clippings invaded the can. They also needed manual removal, and no doubt made their contribution to the germ population. Add to this the chipped baked-enamel billy cans, rings of old milk scum inside the billies, dirty milk boxes, billies without lids, and boxes without doors, where spiders, caterpillars, cats and dogs could sample the milk, and you can see the fallacy of rejecting milk bottles. The milk certainly tasted or was colored differently.

That was my way of life for one and a half years. Imagine what kind of a schoolteacher I must have been. I was constantly lethargic, and no doubt cranky. I can clearly remember times when I put my head on my table to snatch a few minutes rest, and could hear kindly pupils through my daze, whispering, "Sh – Sir's asleep." My room was the quietest in the school for a short while. I always found time to spend with my own children, not enough for my satisfaction, but as much as I could manage. They gave me the impetus, reasons and encouragement to continue.

I know you are curious as to whether I was ever privileged to experience the fantasized spin-off which milkmen are supposed to enjoy. Perhaps you are innocent about this, but it is a favorite milko's joke. I never did 'make it' with any of my customers. I cannot answer for other milkmen. That's their business, and maybe they 'struck it lucky' with lonely lady milk drinkers. I did receive some bottles of beer and cakes for Christmas as symbols of thanks, but I was never propositioned. How could I have taken advantage of any offers of comfort with a lifestyle such as mine   That is why I said earlier, that should my destiny be consignment to hell, I will be delivering milk throughout the eternal night, moonlighting. My real punishment will be facing seduction by sexy young angels, or should that be demons, and be too damned tired to accept.

TRANSITION

Now listen to me, the message is plain,
I'm saying it once, and not tell you again.
Some folk are like Milkman pursuing his route,
While others lie sleeping, not giving a hoot,
For his frustration, betrayal, loss of faith in the Book,
That leads him astray, but he's caught on a hook.

Just like Sisyphus' labors, routinely driven,
Never changing or leaving the streets he's been given.
There's Horse like Society, capricious and strong,
Obedient and mindless, just moving along,
Dragging a wagon, loaded with stuff,
To dole out to others, until they've enough;
A bovine secretion, all the same milk to drink,

8

Sometimes polluted, like waste in a sink.

Is there a solution to break such a spell?
There is, it's in you, in your being to dwell.
Take a chance, listen carefully, follow the clues,
Open your mind, accept no excuses, in fact don't refuse,
To clear out the channels of doubt for release,
Of your stresses and tensions into remarkable peace.

With great courage and hope, I chose as you see,
To begin a new journey, first stop Cundeelee.

In 1954 I stepped out of my routines in New Zealand to pioneer a government school at Cundeelee, 600 miles inland from Perth, Western Australia, in the Great Victoria Desert. With Christian evangelical fervor, I not only taught the children with Assimilation as the goal, but also I wanted to convert them to my faith. It was the beginning of a challenge to my world view and a transformation of my ignorance and prejudices.

BROTHERS
ROBERT McKEICH
and
TOBY JAMIESON
CUNDEELEE 1975

Chapter Two

CUNDEELEE, THE CHALLENGE

We are surrounded by death. All we eat is dead. Pets and plants die. We encounter road kill. War confronts us. Nature sends storms, fires, earthquakes, tsunamis, floods, droughts, and eruptions to let us know her power. Travel, growing up, changing schools, moving, marriage, children leaving home, loss of job, financial loss, stolen property, ill health, accidents, suicide, and ageing are all forms of death; losses that bring out grief of various kinds and intensities. When we think about it, much of our life is spent in avoiding our death through safety rules and practices, adequate food and rest, being cautious in handling machinery, or just crossing the road.

Although we tend to focus on that which affects us personally, individual death, there are the more subtle elements of social death, and the death of cultures. Australian Aborigines have experienced these kinds of death.

In the light of this universal phenomenon what must we do? Cower and lament, or choose to really live? This is the only life we know, let us live it to the full.

Some people are so concerned with what they think might happen after death that they do not really live. They believe and practice religion, observe taboos, conduct parades and feasts, use symbols, commit to medical strategies, issue warnings, invent body language, create music and poetry, erect monuments, ossuaries and statues, and because death is sacred, they make special buildings to commemorate the dead. A great deal of our behavior is oriented to the fact of death, especially human death.

Theological or philosophical belief systems, all culturally different throughout the world, attempt to explain the meaning of human life, the divisions or unity of the human being, and the destiny of the person or the soul after death.

Except in the myths, no-body has revived from being truly dead, or if it appears that they have, they later died again or were removed to another transcendental realm.

I shall tell you about an experience of death that I had at Cundeelee. I give it to you in three parts because it is so complex and important. Listen carefully to what I now say. That's what the Aborigines told me to do.

In the early 1950s I was a missionary school teacher at Cundeelee situated in the Western Desert, 200 miles east of Kalgoorlie, 600 miles from Perth, Western Australia. My tasks were to teach school and to evangelize. Being a curious person I gradually penetrated cultural barriers, especially as I began learning *Wangkai*, their language. At that time they lived in *miamias* scattered within a camping area. A family lived in each bough shelter, with a canvas tarpaulin, and sometimes corrugated iron protection, the center of attention being the small fire at the entrance. As you will see, the fire was not just for heating, it had significant social and symbolic status. Aboriginal fires are something special to experience. They are more than just 'fires'. They have a life, a soul that integrates itself into the individual and social beings of the people. Family relationships are cemented around the fire at each *miamia*, and intimate and often sacred "Law" business is quietly discussed.

For the Aborigines the business of life and death is tied up within their creation and fertility stories and ceremonies, derived from The Dreaming, *Tjukurpa*, their transcendental source of reality. Dying and death are a continuous part of the whole of life. Past, present and future exist together, not in linear form, but all at once, in an ever-present 'now'. It has been called 'Everywhen'. Their relationship with their land, and their kinship structure play significant roles in their daily and ceremonial life, and they come together at the time of death.

They don't have a theology as such. They had no counterpart to our ideas of a God of love and vengeance. We tried to teach them about God and Jesus, but it didn't seem to work. During a visit in their camp one afternoon after I had been at Cundeelee for two years I tried to induce the Aborigines to give me information about some of their ceremonies, thinking that the closeness to them which I had recently experienced was a license to open up these topics. They avoided responding by making subtle changes in the direction of our communication.

As a teacher and a missionary, I was somewhat annoyed and frustrated with the manipulation of events, especially when I was the one usually in control. On the mission compound, and especially in school, I was in charge and could give the orders, or direct the line of conversation, but here in their own domain, they held the power. I was tempted to get up and walk home, but as I gazed around, I saw that the Aborigines were not perturbed by my trespassing upon forbidden topics. Their gracious acceptance of this ignorant *walypala* calmed my emotions. I remember I had to laugh at myself later for my apparently overbearing and arrogant behavior.

At the camp, without realizing it, I was being moved closer toward the outskirts of the camp as we visited several *miamias*. Whenever I got up to go, someone accompanied me to the next group, which I thought was a nice gesture of friendship. However, when I found myself approaching the fire around which the old men sat, my mind felt dazed from gazing into the fires, or the intense concentration required to follow the conversations in *Wangkayi*. I lost track of time. It was the strangest feeling. Little did I know that I was being prepared for the events which soon were to open up.

I had been looking for Toby, my classificatory "brother", throughout this visit, and now about an hour later, he was here, sitting by one of the fires. I dropped down beside him. Not being sure of the time, or how long I had been in the camp, I wanted to glance at my watch, but felt compelled not to do so.

"You wanna know the time?" Toby asked, and I wondered how he had read my thoughts, or maybe it was just a coincidence. "Time got nothin' to do with this business. This Dreaming business . . . and time got nothin' to do with it." From the repetition I gathered that the words were used for emphasis.

There was a long silence. Smoke from the fire blew over me, but like the Aborigines who had lived with open fires since the beginning, I did not move from the discomfort. I was learning in small ways that I must bend to nature, and neither avoid it nor fight it. In these respects I was becoming more Aboriginal.

We were entering into a no-time situation. I gazed into the fire, as they all did, sitting knee to knee, touching and yet not touching. A vibrancy, difficult to identify, began to enter my being. A diffused excitement, an ecstasy, a tension. Sounds romantic, and I suppose it was. I felt as if I had been taken over, and far from being upset about it, I welcomed it, even though I had a flash thought that this might be of the devil. Why should I always think like that?

"We wanna ask you some questions. 'Bout Jesus an' God." It was Toby who spoke. The old men murmured their approval, causing me to wonder once more how much English they understood but were hiding from me. I also thought about my very recent efforts in the camp at initiating conversations about Christianity, and the refusal by the

14

Aborigines to allow me to do so. It was all very strange. This would be the very first time that any Aboriginal had voluntarily asked me such questions. The messages had always been one way.

When I began to speak Toby interrupted. "We bin lis'nin' to you, an' all the other missionaries, an' there are lots a things we doan' unnerstan'." Toby looked down into the burning coals and paused. No-one spoke. We all waited.

Old Thomas suddenly sat up straight, leaned forward and gazed steadfastly into my eyes. His deep-set brown eyes, red from years of smoke and dust, seemed to penetrate my soul. I wanted to look away but could not. I studied the old man's face, stubbly with half grown whiskers, lined from age and exposure to the elements, wide nostrils, and dark skin tinged with red, possibly the remnants of red ochre from a ceremony. Today his *yakirri* of fair human hair instead of red wool made his broad high forehead look distinguished and elegant. Although he was almost bald, his graying hair showed that once it was wavy. There was a strong sense of dignity in the aged man, a powerful impression of composure, and the relaxed body of a person at peace with himself. I was impressed, and wondered how I would look when I reached that age. As I write these words, long after the event, I think I do look like him.

Thomas raised one hand to command silence, and reached out with the other to place it on my knee, like a priest giving a blessing. In a firm voice, unusual for such an old man, he spoke these words in English, surprising me because I thought that he knew only *Wangkayi*.

"Listena me. *Kulila*. I wanna tell you somethin' an' you gotta pay attention." He paused for breath and perhaps to gather his thoughts. "Someday we make you one with us. Mebbe soon, mebbe longa time. You gotta be ready." A long silence followed, his hand still raised in command, his intense eyes holding mine. "When you ready, you will speak for us - in proper English. You will teach many whitefellas, and some *Wangkayi*, and some half way people. Tell 'em 'bout our Law. Tell 'em 'bout our land. Tell 'em 'bout our people b'fore it's too late. You're the teacher."

That wasn't in my thinking at the time, but he proved to be correct, as 21 years later I was taken to sacred ground and initiated into the 'Law' to become a white Aboriginal, and then participated in sacred ceremonies. I also completed my degree in Anthropology and taught classes at the University of Western Australia, the Western Australian Institute of Technology, and universities in America. Some of these classes included courses on the Australian Aborigines.

Thomas breathed heavily after this speech, but carried on with the thought. "We try to tell them how we feel an' no-one listens. Gov'nment people come an' talk, talk, talk, but they doan' wanna know what the *Wangkayi* think. Takes a long time to get the dirt out of their ears . . . an' the mud from their eyes. We got plenty to say, an' one day they will listen to our voices. Meantime you gotta get them ready . . . then you can fade away."

I shifted my position on the ground and lowered my eyes. Thomas barked at me. "Lookame in the eyes. Do you *ninti*? No, I see you doan' unnerstan'. One day it'll come to you. Doan' forget. You speak first, an' later my own people will wake them up." He placed the raised hand on my other knee and squeezed hard with both hands. I could not move. It was as if the old man had entered my being. He remained for a moment and then he was gone.

Thomas looked away to Toby and nodded. Toby sighed, and I felt he too had shared in my experience. Hesitatingly, Thomas continued to speak. "You tell us 'bout Betjlehem, an' Natjareth, an' Tjerutjalem, an' Etjipt. Is that your country, where you come from?"

"No," I replied, having difficulty in concentrating. "I came from New Zealand. It's not far from Australia. I was born there. I might go back there when my work here is finished."

"Your work here never finish." Another old man, Frank, had

suddenly interjected, leaning forward almost aggressively and pointing a finger at me, close to my face. "You go soon from Cundeelee, but you never leave here."

Toby took over. "So these other places you talk about . . . they're like spirit homes . . . where your soul is . . . where everything began, eh?" he inquired.

By now we had been joined by several more Aborigines, men of all ages. Some sat in the circle close to the small fire, while others stood or sat just outside. Quietness pervaded the group. Even the dogs seemed to be engaged in watching and listening. I felt as if I was being put on trial. How could I explain the special meanings of New Zealand, my home country, and the Holy Land? In my preaching and Bible studies with the Aborigines, I had taken for granted that these basic concepts would be understood. The message was what counted. But there seemed to be a point to the questions which I had not yet grasped.

"I suppose that's right. There's one place where my home is, or used to be. Where I was born. And there's the other where my understanding of Jesus is located." I felt as if this was a lame answer and I needed to explain further. "Bethlehem, Jerusalem, Samaria, Galilee, and the other places are where Jesus did his wonderful things, where He did miracles, where He changed peoples' lives."

I waited and waited for some feedback from the Aborigines but there was none. They all sat at the fire absorbed in their own thoughts, and what those could be I wasn't able to guess. I blurted out in desperation, "It's like this. I can live anywhere, in New Zealand, or Australia, but it's from Palestine, the Holy Land where my spiritual life, my *kurrti*, has come. The stories help me to know God and what He wants from me."

I was getting frustrated. These people were not helping me to make sense. It was easy to be in charge, to preach or teach on my own territory, or to give out prepared words, but here I felt exposed to my ignorance. Finally I said, almost

17

in desperation, "Why do you want to know all this? We've been telling you about it since we've been here. This isn't new to you."

The old men began muttering together, words which I could not catch, but which I knew all the others understood. My confidence was shaken, I felt in the minority, and did not like it. There was no animosity in their demeanor; in fact some gave a faint smile when I caught their eyes. I relaxed a little. I had come to Cundeelee to lead these folk to Christ, but I got the strong impression that they were going to lead me in the direction which they themselves chose. Toby spoke again.

"We're jus' like you. This place, Cundeelee, is where we live, but this not our country. Our spirits are in another place. That's where our life comes from. We have stories of how an' where things were made, how they came to be the way they are, and we mus' tell the stories to our children, jus' like you do with Jesus. But we doan' unnerstan' why we have to believe your stories are better'n ours. You doan' tell us anythin' new. Jus' a different way to say the same thing." Toby looked a little embarrassed at what he had just said, but the soft murmuring from the group supporting him encouraged him to continue.

"You know that we were taken from our own country and brought to Cundeelee. Your people took our land from us, an' killed our families. Now you take our children up to the mission, an' won't let us teach them our ways. We're not angry, only sad. *Ngarlturriwa.* You're killing us bit by bit." I began to protest, although I really did not know what I could say. "I never did that . . . I don't want to do that . . . it's best for the children to become assimilated and move into Australian society . . . this place is better than the bush where you used to live . . ." I trailed off, searching for something to say which would redeem my position as a missionary school teacher, but I could not find the right words. My response sounded stupid, mere excuses, almost judgmental,

18

unreasonable justifications for my own actions and those of my colleagues and forbears.

Another long silence ensued. Toby spoke again, very quietly and without malice. "As usual you doan' unnerstan'." His voice was gentle, as if talking to a child. "We wan' you to know how we feel. Your people, the white people, came here and took what you wanted, never asking if it belonged to anyone - our land. You took our women, you took our children, you killed us, you took our language, you left us with nothing but memories. When you took our land you killed our spirits, which is worse than killing our people. We know. We are not living in our land, our own country. You shifted us an' we died. Our bodies died, and our spirits died. We were taken from *Kulkopin* and *Tjuntjuntjarra* and our other special places. We thought maybe that the stories of Jesus would give us our life back, but they no good for the *Wangkayi*. Mebbe they be good for you, but they doan' make much sense to us. Your stories belong to another land, our stories belong to our land. We are like the trees. You see only withered leaves and dry branches, but our roots run deep in the land, waiting for us to water them with our *inma*, our ceremonies. They wait for our spirits to mak'em new. In 'tween time, we die."

Old Thomas slowly and deliberately leaned toward the fire, reached out and from the blaze took a short fire stick. The tip glowed dark red with a small, dynamic, dancing flame. He held it high for all to see, and in an instant plunged it deep into the dead ashes at the perimeter of the fire, extinguishing the living flame.

A long silence followed. No one moved. It was an eternity in a moment. The symbolic message was obvious.

I thought I had to say something. Nothing came. My evangelical zeal remained strong and I wanted to justify what we were doing to the Aborigines. Doubts slowly challenged me, and then my mind began racing. There were many in my world for whom these Biblical sacred words, and the significance of their meanings, were absolutely fundamental to their faith . . . their living faith. But for some reason, which I did not yet understand, they were not appealing to these Aboriginal people in the same way. I knew this was why they brought me to their fires today. In my optimism and perhaps to justify my role at Cundeelee, I thought they would want to believe as I did, but something in their view and understanding of the world made it difficult for them to do so.

I realized that it was not the devil blinding their eyes, nor their stubbornness, evil spirits, sin, or debaucheries which were the stumbling blocks in their inability to accept my particular theology. We had judged them on these. The Biblical message was attractive to me, but related to a distant foreign culture, a patriarchal tribal system found among pastoralists, in another land, and with an historical background in a totally different context.

A couple of thoughts briefly entered my mind for the first time, perhaps 'messages', to inform me, that what we took for granted in our society was 'foreign' to this culture. I had been so ethnocentric that it had not dawned on me that I had ignored the Aboriginal world view in pursuing my own evangelical agenda. For example, the Bible story of the wise man building his house on a rock and the foolish man building on sand was totally reversed here in the desert. Nomadic people, who slept on the ground, found it was comfortable to sleep on the sand and foolish to find rocky beds. We quoted with confidence, 'though your sins be as scarlet, they shall be as white as snow; though they be red like crimson, they shall be as wool'. The imagery was clear to us, but not understood by the Aborigines who never experienced snow, and who saw sheep as dirty brown. Scarlet and crimson were sacred colors to the Aborigines, especially in their art and body painting, very positive and not associated with sin. These were inappropriate metaphors when in the context of the Aboriginal environment and culture.

Toby woke me from my reverie. "We try to unnerstan' an' believe what you say. We already knew everything before you came. We fitted in with everything around us, an' were comfortable. The guv'nment came along, it sent you, it pays you to civilize us. You all part of that. But we civilized. Always have bin. You wanna save us from our sins, but we had no sins until you arrived. What you call sins you gavem to us, an' then you tell us they bad. Gettin' drunk, smokin', buyin' our women, fightin' - we never much fight before, or neglectin' our children. You took our kids away, an' we have no families any more. You wanna teach us to pray. We gotta do things like bow our heads an' talk out loud. You confuse us by makin' us use special words you doan' use anywhere else. You tell us to pray with our hearts or God won' hear us. When we pray, an' God doesn' give us what we pray for, you say we are to blame. How do we know if we are praying right, an' if God really does hear us? Sometimes you say that God does not want to give us what we pray for - like rain - an' we're confused. Why doesn' God wanna give us rain? You always have an answer, but we wonder if you be lyin' 'bout all this. Do you know what we think? This is God's air, this is God's sky, this is God's land, these are God's animals an' plants, an' we are God's people. Jus' livin' is an act of prayer."

Toby paused, breathing heavily after such a long speech. I had no reply. They had come asking for answers, but I had none. Merely repeating the scriptures was useless, not because they lacked rationality or power, but because they lacked context. The lives of these people were tied into a different world view. I had a vague insight, that I might find these people were closer to God than I had imagined. I needed to ask them more questions, so I could answer their questions.

Once again Toby spoke. He was struggling to present the fundamentals of the Aboriginal ethos. "We were made here. The *Wangkayi* were always here. We have always bin here since Dreaming. This is our country, even though you won' let us live in our own land. We are people of this land. What you're doing to the land you're doing to us. When you destroy the land you destroy us. Give us back our land an' you give us back our life. We know God, we bin know him for a longa time, mebbe a differen' way to believe, an' a little differen' way to see'um, but we be close to everything he made, an' he be close to us."

Well, I was impressed too. As if to cover my self-consciousness, I began to rise to my feet. I suddenly realized that my bladder was near bursting. One of the men reached out and helped me, the gesture being one of comradeship, almost love. I watched the men move away to their own *miamias*, and noticed that the old men were now lying down on their mattresses close to the fire. I felt the aching muscles in my back from sitting so long in the cold. I found my own spot to relieve myself, and skirting the camp, made my way wearily toward the mission.

I was a little stunned. Much had been said in that brief encounter. The word 'brief' hit me. I really had no idea of how long it had lasted, and now it did not seem to matter. The challenge had been given to me by these so-called simple people. I had been reminded that these Aborigines had deep emotions and thoughts about what was happening to them, and they wanted to make some sense out of the impact of the alien invasion of their land, including that of the mission upon their lives. Toby had said that they were going to talk about timeless things, about the Dreaming, and I had caught a glimpse of what he meant.

I was startled to feel an arm around my shoulder. Toby had again come silently up to me, touching my inner being as well as my body. We parted without words at the edge of the mission compound. Toby silently walked away.

1975 CUNDEELEE ABORIGINAL FAMILY
GATHERED AROUND CAMP FIRE

Chapter Three

CUNDEELEE, AN OLD MAN DIES

D ying is just part of the life processes. It is expected but not welcomed. The Aboriginal kinship system, and their ways of caring for each other, made life comfortable for every member of the group. Everyone was related to everyone else and they behaved accordingly. Each individual had a role to play. Death interrupted the flow of daily activities, changed the reciprocal expectations of the society, and made a huge dent in the social system. Underpinning the tragedy of death were the myths and rituals handed down since the beginning, originating in *Tjukurpa,* The Dreaming.

A week after my dramatic experience in the camp my four children John, 12, Miriam, 11, Paul, 6, and Julie Ann, 4 and I had been out for a walk in the bush, something we did several times a week. The bush claimed you. It got into your soul, your being, and in a peaceful way promoted communion with Nature. We unwound from the mission stresses that way. Betty had returned to New Zealand for several months having found the conditions at Cundeelee too much for her health.

When we arrived back at the mission, the sad news that old Thomas had died took away much of our happiness. While Andy, one of the young missionaries, mentioned him by name, the Aboriginal children called him *Tjamu* or *Tjilpi,*

'Grandfather' or 'Old One', endearing terms used for the aged, statements of a close relationship and respectful behavior, and the means by which the saying of his name could be avoided. When a person dies, out of respect, their name is never mentioned again. The Aborigines believe their spirit is still around and could cause harm.

That old man had delivered the message to me at the camp fire, and although I had thought about the words, I did not yet fully appreciate their meaning. Perhaps they were just the words of a senile old man, a threat, or a prophecy. How I could teach Aborigines about Aboriginal ways did not make sense. How I could leave here and yet not leave here, as Frank had said, was a mystery, unless the physical leaving was of a different kind from the spiritual one.

I decided to visit the camp to pay my respects, approaching the camp cautiously and with reverence, would ask permission to enter, and follow whatever behavior seemed appropriate, leaving if they asked me to.

I left my children at home with some school work to do, and headed up the hill passing by the school. Wally, the mission superintendent, and Andy, the young missionary, were standing in the slowly fading light, talking about the recent death. Joining them, I remarked that I was walking down to the camp to pay my respects. Immediately Wally reacted. His tone became dogmatic and commanding, which set me back.

"It'd be wise for you to stay away. You've no idea of the bad things that are going on. Don't go down there." He was giving orders, and obviously expected me to obey. However, I was not going to give in so easily.

"What sorts of things do you mean?" I asked, trying hard to control my growing resentment.

"They're taking all their clothes off, cutting themselves, wailing and ranting, and possibly doing sexual things. It's disgusting. Stay away." Wally had a hard edge to his voice. Andy nodded in agreement.

I thought for a moment, and then quietly said, "Old Thomas was a special friend to me. I liked him. At least I ought to show my face for a moment. I owe the Aborigines that."

Wally was beginning to lose his composure. Wagging his finger at me, he shouted, "You're spending too much time with the Aborigines. Your job is in the school. Attend to your business there. An' . . . an' . . . an' you'll soon be thinking that their sins are quite OK. They have a way of getting at you. They're bloody subtle you know."

Wally stopped suddenly, knowing that he had spoken the expletive common to Australians, but taboo to good people like himself.

It was this small trigger which made me more determined than ever to visit the camp. Calmly I replied, "I'll take that risk. I'm going."

It was a choice I needed to make, and one that continued to change my life. As I turned to walk slowly and deliberately down the hill, following the trail to the camp, Wally, shaking with anger, shouted after me, "The Aborigines don't want you there. They'll kick you out." As I trudged on he threw out an afterthought, "They might spear you. Watch out. I warned you." Finally, a pathetic demand which had already lost its power, "Come back here at once." He made a move in my direction, but Andy took him by the arm and turned him back to the mission compound.

Walking the mile of well beaten track, made smooth by the passage of many bare feet over the past few months, I had time to reflect on what Wally had just said. Perhaps I would not be welcome, but I always seemed to be. That was under normal conditions, and this was a special circumstance. I resolved to be sensitive to the Aboriginal mood, and come away if I thought it best.

As I neared the camp, I heard the wailing of many voices, accompanied by the barking of dozens of dogs. I took the most open part of the trail so that I would become visible fairly quickly. No one seemed to notice me, so I stopped at the edge of the camp and waited. I could see many of the fires had been put out, several of the *miamias* had been torn down as if a hurricane wind had blown through, and some people were running around the area seemingly aimlessly, while others sat huddled and bent over, their hands covering their faces. The wailing came from those sitting down. In the slowly fading light, I noticed that a few of the men and women were naked. I called out in a loud voice, the 'cooee' sound used in the Australian outback. No one paid attention. Then I saw Toby walking toward me.

"Whattja waitin' there for? Come on in. Bill's already here." Toby was so matter of fact that I was at first surprised. "This not what you're used to, but this the way we do it. Some of these people *ngampu yartaka*. They be naked just like ol' times, but it's no shame."

Bill was the missionary carpenter from Canada, and the fix-it man. He had grown closer to the Aborigines by his open mindedness and acceptance of their ways. Despite being such a small isolated community I never saw much of him, and I knew he and Wally did not get along together. "Is it OK if I come in?" I asked very tentatively.

"Sure. Wish more missionaries would come. They say they sorry an' that's it. They wanna giv'm a Christian funeral. I think it's ta stop our ways. You people doan' unnerstan' nothin'." There was no malice or animosity, merely the statement of what he thought.

"I just want to let you know that I'm *ngarlturriwa*, really sorry for the old man." After Toby's implied admonition for the apparent lack of caring by the missionaries, I felt as if my words lacked sincerity, even though I meant them to be. Toby did not seem to notice.

"D'ya wanna seeum? The old man?" Toby was already leading me out of the camp to where Thomas had so recently had his fire. The fire was out, and I was reminded of the fire stick which had been extinguished before my eyes as a symbol of death. At first I could not see the body because

28

of the small crowd of people who were gathered around it. There were men and women, some naked and some in torn clothing, obviously rent as a demonstration of their grief. The nakedness did not give me any concern. Also I did not find the presence of little children in the group to be out of place, even though some of them were holding the dead man's hand, and some were stroking his forehead. Most were quietly sobbing, with tears of grief streaking their cheeks. I noticed that several men and women had gashes on their foreheads from which blood was oozing, or had dried into black lines. The upper arms and breasts of several showed lacerations and blood.

My gaze drifted to the still form lying on the ground. He was wrapped in a blanket except for his chest and head. The lines of age were gone from his face, and although he still appeared to be quite thin, he was not as emaciated as I remembered him. An unusual red glow on the dark skin, from a thin layer of red ochre, gave him the appearance of good health. For the first time I could clearly see the *mirna*, the initiation scars on his chest. They were about half an inch wide and ran from side to side in parallel lines, three of them. Following Toby's example, I sat down beside the old man as people moved over for me. Strangely I did not find it difficult to cry. Crying was not out of place here, and soon I was sobbing like the others.

Gazing at the body lying there I could not stop my thoughts: This old man had lived for many years, how many I could only guess, and now his life was through. Others would carry on the traditions for him. Men like Toby would continue with the language and the stories, and maybe the ceremonies. They would uphold the kinship system, and the rules for good behavior. Or would they?

With the death of this man, who began his life back in the country where his spirit originated, something was lost, forever. What had he been able to communicate before he died? More significantly, what did the people in the camp really know of traditional *Wangkayi* ways? How much had they never been taught, or did not want to learn, or through the efforts of *walypalas* like myself, been deliberately deprived of. What about the children on the mission? By isolating them from their parents, teaching them in school, and imposing Christianity upon them, the goals of assimilation might be achieved, but at what cost?

I felt as if I was weeping for more than just this old man. I was beginning to see that my tears were for an almost extinct culture, represented here by *Tjamu*, Grandfather.

I felt Toby gently touching me on the shoulder. "Gotta go now. Things to tell you. Come."

I reluctantly arose, as if my work here beside the body had not been completed.

"We find Bill. Together we 'splain some things you gotta know."

Bill was sitting alone, alongside a derelict *miamia*, the ashes of a dead fire giving off the faintest wisp of smoke as if to say, 'This is the spirit of the once-alive fire, now dead.' He had taken off his shirt, and I could see red ochre glistening on his back and chest. He called to me. "Come on mate. Siddown here. We've got some talking to do. We knew that you'd come tonight. Have any trouble getting here? . . . no . . . don't answer that."

Both Toby and I eased ourselves to the ground. I found myself facing the center of the camp, and was pleased in that I could watch what was going on. It was almost dark, the people becoming mere shadows at every moment. This was the strangest camp situation which I had ever experienced, as if everything alive was slowly dying as I watched it.

"Are your kids all right?" asked Bill. "If not we'd better get going."

I reassured him by saying, "They're pretty capable of looking after themselves. They're good kids."

"We can sen' a woman from here to look after 'em if you like. What about my woman, Evelyn?" added Toby, indicating a

30

concern for the children which was so common among these people.

"No, they're OK. Thanks anyway," I said gratefully.

Whereas the Aborigines were always slow to get going, which was their way of doing business, or carrying on a conversation, Bill jumped right in to the topic. "Toby wants me to fill you in on some of the things going on round here. He thinks I can put it better than he can. I don't agree because it's their business, but he'll help me out."

I raised my hand to ask for a pause. "First of all let me ask you a question - some questions. Why you, Bill? Why not the other missionaries who have been here longer than you? And now why me? They seem to have chosen me for something, I'm not sure what."

Both Bill and Toby looked at each other before Toby answered for him. "Some people kinda special. They getta know *Wangkayi* people an' doan' boss us aroun'. They try to unnerstan' *Wangkayi* ways without keepin' on tellin' us we always sinnin'. Bill one special man - you another. You doan' unnerstan' jus' yet. Bit by bit you'll *ninti*."

He paused for a moment and Bill added, "You know that as soon as I finish the building project I'm working on I'll be leaving Cundeelee for Canada, and won't be back. The *Wangkayi* know that too. You've got to do something for them. They trust you. If you do the right thing by them, they'll always respect you, although others, especially the Christian missionaries and the church, will judge and misjudge you. They won't understand. You'll be true to your faith, I know that, even though it will change. Enough of that for now. No. Just one more thing. Pretty soon you'll be going away from Cundeelee, but you'll not be really leaving. You'll be taking something of Cundeelee with you, and you'll be coming back."

This last statement was what I had been told so very recently by Frank. I was beginning to understand what it meant, and hearing it again from Bill sent a shiver down my back.

31

"Back to business. Toby wants me to tell you about how life goes in circles. He doesn't say it that way, but that's what it is." He looked at Toby and Toby looked at him, nodding in approval. "I'll make it simple, but nothing like this is simple, so bear with me. It's taken me time to put these ideas together, and Toby and I have frequently discussed them. I can't tell you some of the details, because much of this is related to the secret life, men's business."

"You lissena him," Toby broke in. "He not a proper *Wangkayi*, but pretty close. Bill jus' a boy, a *tjitji*, not yet a man, but he almos' a wati. You a *tjitji* too. One day you be a *wati*, a man. We see to that. Now lissena him."

Bill continued as if the interruption had not occurred, but I was puzzled about the meaning of what Toby had said.

Bill spoke, "This isn't exactly right, but they don't see a direct connection between sexual intercourse and making babies. They rationalize it this way, that if sex made babies, then each sexual act would produce a child. It doesn't, so there must be something else which gets a woman pregnant. Remember, we know the biology but they don't. I'm really starting at the wrong end, but these comments set the stage for their reality, which is quite different from ours. Yet, in some respects, it's not that much different from our own claims that God gives us our children. A spirit child enters the mother from *Tjukurrpa*, the Dreaming. The man merely opens the way, so intercourse is necessary to let the spirit in. Do you follow me?" He looked at me and at Toby.

Bill continued. "Well, the first thing to understand is that each baby, each child, each adult is not so much a physical person as a spiritual one. When we deal with the *Wangkayi* we are dealing primarily with spiritual beings." He paused to let that idea sink in. "Don't ever forget that, and you'll be truly giving these people the dignity and respect they deserve. A pity we don't apply that concept to all people throughout the world."

"The mother makes the body for the spirit," proffered Toby.

"When it's ready out it comes."

"Takes nine months to do that," added Bill. "Nine months to clothe the spirit with a body so it can live in this world."

"I like that idea," I said, "Go on,".

"Well, the child grows and passes through several stages in its life. Each significant one has a ritual or ceremony, and many of these are secret. But in order to be part of the society, to be allowed to participate, to marry, have children, lead in important matters, every child must go through what is called the Law to become an adult. It's different for males and females." When he paused, Toby leaned over to him, touched him on the knee, and then wagged his finger at Bill. Bill smiled at him saying, "It's OK. I won't tell any secrets." Toby leaned back in trust, and nodded for Bill to continue.

Bill went on, "At the end of life, where we are tonight, there's a ceremony to return the spirit to where it came from, back to *Tjukurrpa*. Actually there are two ceremonies. I'll come to that in a moment. In our Christian churches there are many arguments as to where the spirit of a person goes when they die, not only where but when. Who's right? Does the spirit go straight to heaven or hell, or does it go to an intermediary place? Does it remain dormant until the resurrection, or is this life the end? Is there a second chance for those who miss out on heaven? That's what's confusing to people like the Aborigines, because we ourselves don't have a single clear-cut, agreed-upon answer. But they have their own beliefs, which are why we're not very successful with putting ours across."

Bill said, "Tomorrow you will attend the funeral . . ."

At this point I interrupted. "I'll be in school tomorrow. I can't go to the funeral."

"Then why're you here tonight?" asked Toby, for the first time with tones of resentment in his voice. "We thought you cared. You jus' like the rest of 'em."

Bill gently raised his hand to silence Toby. "No Toby, he's new to all of this. We've got to teach him. Work's different for a *walypala*. He thinks his work in school is most important. We think the work going on here is more important still." A long pause ensued to allow Toby to calm down . . . and for me to rethink what I had said. Bill spoke again.

"This is important, not only for you but for the school children. They've got to know their own Aboriginal ways of dealing with death, in addition to the Christian way. Wally may not allow them to attend the *Wangkayi* service, but you mustn't be the one to stop them. The Aboriginal service, or rather 'ceremony', is much more complex than I can say here, and if you're there it will help you to understand what I'm going to tell you now. It doesn't matter if you believe me, or believe the *Wangkayi*, it's what they themselves believe which is important in these circumstances. This man over there has been with them for many years, not merely his body but his spirit. It came to his mother, grew a body, lived a long life, and now lies waiting for the next step. Do you follow me?"

I could not find the appropriate words, and so remained silent. I made sense of what I was hearing, but it did not exactly conform to my own understanding of the life process.

"Toby, do you want to go on from here, or shall I tell him?"

"No. You tell'm. You doin' OK."

"Well, tomorrow you'll see only the beginning of a funeral. I'll leave the details for you to see for yourself. Remember that the spirit has been tied to the body for many years, and doesn't want to leave the body with which it has been comfortable. It doesn't want to leave the people, the family, the children and grandchildren, and other kin in this community, so it stays around here at Cundeelee. One sad thing is that it would rather be at the traditional spirit center which is far away to the north east, in the true home country. That's where all the Cundeelee people would rather be, but that's another issue. These displays of grief are not only a way of dealing with their emotions; they are ways of showing the spirit of the dead person that they care. The wailing and cutting, dousing the fires, destroying the *miamias*, are evidence to the spirit that they are sorry, *ngarlturriwa*, for it leaving. There is a big difference between our funerals and this one. The grave is not filled in. They leave it open for the spirit to come and go and visit the body. Of course the body disintegrates. After nine months to a year they perform another ceremony in which the spirit takes its last look at the body . . ."

Toby interrupted, finishing the description. "It looks at the body, now just bones, an' says 'This one not my body. I useta have nice skin an' meat. That a no-good one, not mine.' An' the spirit now ready to go away to *Tjukurrpa*."

Bill waited, in case he wanted to continue, and when he did not, Bill courteously asked him, "Shall I go on? We're nearly finished."

Toby nodded yes, and whispered, "*Yuwa*."

"This is an interesting observation. Notice that it takes nine months to put on the flesh, and about nine months to take it off. Everything is perfect." Bill sat back and relaxed.

"Wow!" I whispered. "It's all so neat. What a fantastic idea. I really can't comment. I'm stunned. It all makes sense doesn't it?"

"There's just one more thing. It's about the red ochre. May I tell him about that Toby, or will you?" Bill was sensitive to this aspect of Aboriginal Law and did not want to give offense. However, with the ochre so obvious on the dead man, and his own upper body covered with red ochre, he thought that I should know what it represented.

"Best if I tell'm. Pretty scary stuff, an' some of it secret, but OK to tell this." Toby paused in the way typical of the *Wangkayi*. "Well, when a baby's born it covered with blood. Blood the sign of life. Always the sign of life. Important too in other *inma*, what you call'm corroboree. This time the old man being born again. He gotta die so's he can live a new life. We all gotta die or we stay like caterpillars an' never learn to fly like butterflies. He not really dead, he jus' goin' into another life. Red ochre, *walka*, is the blood we put on for him to giv'm a proper new birth. Bill got'm on too, an' me." He pulled open his shirt to show me.

There was a covering of red dust on Toby's chest, and I saw the patterns of long scars from an initiation ceremony earlier in his youth. What pain he must have endured to receive those? I was mesmerized by them, wanted to reach out to touch them, to feel if they were real, and wondered whether I would be able to endure such a test if I were called upon to do so. Toby reached out and touched me on the knee. "You want'm? You want'm too?" Toby continued. "We put *walka* on you if you like. Take your shirt off. We got some here. You doan' hafta, but we got some."

Without hesitation, I found myself unbuttoning my shirt and taking it off. Toby produced a tobacco can from his back pocket and twisted off the lid. He handed the can to Bill who took a small quantity of the red dust on to his fingers and began smearing it on my back. Toby did the same on my chest until a red glow shone over my white skin. Perhaps it was merely the unfamiliar touching, or it may have been the ceremonial act, but I felt a glow within myself as well. This was the first time I had made an act of identification with these people, at least in such a practical way. Knowing something of its symbolic meaning, gave support to the ritual. Little did I know that it was the beginning of a new birth for myself. I would move deeper into the Law than what was happening to me at this time, and the same glow of emotion would enable me to endure more than this imagined pain of chest scars.

When they had finished smearing me with red ochre my thoughts darted from one idea to another. 'In a birth, the child does nothing but allows itself to be born. In death the body is acted upon, it cannot act for itself. In baptism the candidate places himself in the hands of the minister during the immersion and return to life. People submit to the authority of others at a wedding. Now I am allowing myself to be covered with symbolic blood in order to share something with that dear old man over there.' These were powerful thoughts.

"Toby smiled broadly, his white teeth showing in the darkness. He approved of Bill's description of these matters, and he was delighted with my understanding, but most of all he was filled with satisfaction that I had allowed myself to share in this ritual, the beginning of a series of events which would be good for me, and best of all, good for the *Wangkayi*. We sat still for some time until Toby, his sensitivity to others showing through, suggested that we should put on our shirts and go to our homes.

On the way, Bill explained that they would all be moving camp tomorrow after the body had been taken away, another means of discouraging the spirit of the dead man from doing them harm. The reason why his name was not ever mentioned again, for them moving camp, and for conducting the ceremonies in the proper way, was to show full respect to the deceased, and to ensure that he would not use his new powers, free from the body, to bring upon the living any danger, disease, or accident. Finally, in around nine months, there would be another ritual for his spirit to return to *Tjukurrpa*, joining his deceased relatives, which would bring the life circle to a close, at least for him.

For me, however, I had just now entered the new life circle. My former 'truths' were still relevant but now subtlely transformed by what I had experienced. First, I recognized that there were other realities beyond my own that made consistent sense to these special people, and could make sense to me if I would let them. My realities were not the only ones. Second, I began to question some of my basic beliefs and practices that I had accepted and defended in the name of Christian Faith. Third, I was here to evangelize the Aborigines into my understanding about God and the World, to make them just like me, but I was awakened to the

37

futility of doing that. They already had a deep spirituality, developed over thousands of years, and not a mere six thousand of Biblical times. I had been told by my church, and had preached, that there were no other alternatives to my truth. To be authentic, I now needed to open my ears and eyes and consider other ways. I was not compelled to commit myself to new thoughts, only think about them.

* * * * * *

Now, years later, things are not the same as they were. Children have grown up and left Cundeelee, and others have died. Everyone has moved, and Cundeelee is no more. Those years at Cundeelee were unique and special occasions, never to be repeated. I was blessed and honored to be part of them. As my own time draws to a close and think about that old man, my Tjamu, I wrote this poem about respect for my body, our partnership in life:

OH BODY, DEAR BODY
(A Conversation)

Oh Body, dear Body,
My only Body, mine,
Why give up on me now?
Why restrict my activity,
For Body you restrict yourself?
You slowed me down,
Ignoring Mind's entreaties.
Oh Body, you and I are one.

Oh Robbie, don't you know,
I have my allotted time to be with you,
To give you all the strength I have;
But I grew tired as the years passed by,
And you tested me well with your living.

Yes, Body, I know about that.

You have been my breathing,
My voice, my hearing,
My taste, smell, touch;
But now these diminish,
Despite all efforts by clever men and women,
To heal you, dear Body, with tubes, artificial substitutes,
Electronic devices, and medications by the score.

Let me remind you, Robbie, that I hiked your trails,
I climbed those hills and swam your ocean waters,
I rode your bicycle and enjoyed the motor cycle too,
I tried your food, both simple and exotic,
I walked your deserts, visited foreign places,
And sat down with you in the Aboriginal camps.
I went to school with you, and read those books;
I fed your brain with nourishment,
So Mind could become the creator,
Even when we slept.

Oh Body, dear Body, my only Body,
I thank you for your faithfulness,
I honor you for your quiet activities,
Of growing me from Babe to Man,
For the wonderful 86 years, with more to go.
What do I owe you for all that?
How much longer will you be with me?

Oh Robbie, you owe me nothing for those years.
I was neither your slave nor your master,
I was your partner in this enterprise of life.
Robbie, you are only you, with me.

I know that, dear Body, and more.
You were my companion through life's trials;
You wept with me when things got tough,

And laughed as pleasures heaped on pleasures.
When Heart balked at living you restored my health.
You joined me in making love,
And generated copies of yourself, dear Body,
Your four children.

Robbie, I gave you sleep, and now I'm tired;
I'm winding down, and need my rest.
Sorry Robbie, I must go soon.
We all have done our part;
For together we created,
Those stories, poems, lectures, photographs,
And journals of our lives, dear Robbie.
Memories that shall live on when I am in the soil.
I must go soon,
But Robbie, I'll be with you to the end.

1975 CUNDEELEE, ROB WITH
ABORIGINAL MEN

<hr>

Chapter Four

CUNDEELEE, A FUNERAL AND BOXES

Early the next morning the sound of the truck engine wakened me around 6.00 a.m.. I had slept heavily all night, and still felt not ready for the day. Noticing that the sheets were tinged with red, I sat up and hastily reached for my shirt. It too was coated on the inside with red dust. Locating another shirt, I washed myself very quickly and got dressed. The noise of the engine gradually diminished as it traveled over the hill toward the camp.

My children were up by the time the truck returned. They stood by the door waiting for it. It was invisible until it rounded the top of the hill by the school and moved toward us. Wally was driving, and on the back were several Aborigines, some standing holding on to the roof of the cab, and several sitting. Only when it came past the house did we notice that a body, entirely wrapped in a gray blanket, was lying on the tray, with a woman supporting the head in her lap to prevent it from bouncing. It passed quickly, heading along the north road toward *Munyurra*, Queen Victoria Springs.

None of the mission Aboriginal children were to be seen. Wally had told Andy to keep them occupied in the dining room, so, as curious as they were, they were singing hymns and choruses when the truck returned from the camp. Despite

Andy's encouragement and threatened punishment, they spontaneously stopped singing as the truck passed through the mission, and then they resumed only halfheartedly when it was gone.

I had discussed the old man's death with my children and found out that they already knew from the other children a great deal about the Aboriginal perspective. They had decided to call him *Tjamu*, Grandfather, just as the Aborigines did. I told them about the actions of the small children in the camp who still lived with their families, and they were comfortable with that.

Half an hour later the truck returned empty, parked near the dormitories, and Wally rang the dinner bell. June, Wally's wife and her boys, with Grace another missionary, and Andy climbed aboard, the women sitting in the cab. The Aboriginal children climbed silently on the back.

Before they could take off, Bill drove up to us in the Jeep, and invited my family to join him. Actually Wally had not discussed any of the arrangements with us, or invited us to attend. Bill pointed out a number of *Wangkayi* walking in the bush past the mission compound. Without a word he drove on, and the mission truck followed. It was about two miles to the burial ground.

Rather than drive right up to the grave site, Bill stopped the Jeep about a hundred yards away, and we got out and walked. Wally, however, drove right on by, and parked close to the prepared area. When the engine stopped, there was a tangible silence. A sign of disapproval. The sacred area had been invaded, violated by Wally driving in.

Everybody, even the usually exuberant Aboriginal children, moved around to their positions without a sound. Wally placed the children near the truck, at some distance from the Aborigines, forbidding them to go to their families. He, with the other missionaries, stood beside the vehicle.

The *Wangkayi* stood or sat, alone or in small groups, around the perimeter of a large circle of cleared ground, about thirty yards in diameter. Bill gave a hand signal to me and we joined the Wangkayi, sitting down close to Toby and his family. This action pleased me greatly, and no doubt pleased the Aborigines also. I felt we were identifying with the Aborigines, sharing the ceremony with them, while Wally glared at us in disapproval, but dared say nothing.

I discreetly looked around. In the center of the huge circular ground, cleared of all vegetation, a grave had been dug with the earth piled alongside. The body was lying, apparently on his back, beside the grave, opposite to the mound. As the Aborigines arrived, they settled into places with traditionally prescribed positions, determined by their relationship with the deceased, and their established place in the wider kinship structure. Although there were some obvious cuts on the foreheads of a few, they had evidently washed off the dried blood. Whereas the school children were seated near the truck, all the missionaries remained standing.

Wally handed a pile of hymn books to his two boys, and they began distributing them to the school children and to the seated *Wangkayi*. When this was done, there being some embarrassment among the Aborigines, he called out in a loud voice for all to bow in prayer. Many of the Aborigines lowered their heads, but some gazed around disinterestedly. The prayer was a mixture of praise to God, some remarks about death, heaven and hell, and a brief sermon on repentance from sins. Following the 'amen', Wally asked them all to turn to a particular number in the hymn book. There was much scuffling of pages, and I was certain that many of the Aborigines only pretended to locate the right page. Wally began singing the hymn, 'Rock of Ages cleft for me', and others joined in as best they could. The hymn became the theme for a sermon on living the right way so that all could reach heaven. Wally emphasized the need to give one's heart to Jesus so that when they drew 'this fleeting breath', when their 'eyelids closed in death' when they 'soared to realms unknown', they would see God

45

on His 'judgment throne', and then it would be too late for repentance. There was no mention of where Wally thought the soul of the old man might be residing.

On three occasions Wally mentioned the old man by name. The Aborigines reacted as if they had been hit, sucked in their breaths, looked embarrassed, and hung their heads. Surely Wally knew the taboo on using the name. He deliberately flung the name in their faces. It was hard to understand. A prayer of benediction concluded the formal service.

Wally moved over to the body, and called upon some Aboriginal men to help him put the corpse into the grave. No one moved. He looked around appealingly and asked for help, but again no one moved. Eventually old Frank, who would be too weak to help, limped over to Wally, and quietly said in very good English, "Christian business now over. You leave him to us. We fix him up OK. Thank you. You can go home now." He placed a hand on Wally's shoulder, gently turned him in the direction of the truck, and subtly but strongly gave him a shove.

Livid with anger, Wally strode to the truck, ordered the school children to climb aboard, and began shepherding them on to the tray. He did not notice two Aboriginal men approaching, and they were upon him when he turned.

"Let the children stay. We not be finish yet. You can stay too if you like. Nothin' secret goin' on here." The words were gentle, appealing, and yet firm.

Wally was somewhat intimidated, but as Andy and June joined him, he regained his composure and his authority, almost spitting out his reply. "No! It's school time and they'll be late. I don't want them around here while you perform your heathen ceremonies. Bury old Thomas now and we'll all go home." Turning away from the men, he continued lifting and pushing children on to the truck.

The Aboriginal men were offended by the use of the name and moved off to join the others.

When they were ready to go, Wally called to Bill and me,

"Come on. Let's go. School starts in thirty minutes."

Well, we had no intention of leaving now, and waved for him to go ahead. With a threatening look Wally slammed the truck door, revved up the engine, and drove away.

Throughout the episode the Aborigines had remained quietly where they were, but now a bustling began, with everyone seeming to have something to do.

Some of the men wandered away, to disappear among the trees. The men and women who remained began breaking branches from nearby eucalyptus trees and piled them alongside the open grave. Toby came over and invited us to do the same. We were delighted to participate, my children included, showing no reticence about approaching the blanketed body. A few people merely sat and observed the activity. The pile grew quite high and each person then took a branch and dropped it into the grave. When the floor had been covered with the fragrant branches, two men climbed in and began to line the sides of the pit with the foliage. Old *Tjamu* was to have a soft aromatic bed on which to lie. At last the job was completed, and all went back to their places to sit and wait. Once again silence pervaded the area, except for the songs of some birds nearby. This was a time for reflection and reverence.

Time passed. In the presence of this old man, now facing eternity, or rather the timelessness of *Tjukurrpa*, time had no meaning. I did not know what the others were thinking, and I wondered what my children were making of this unique experience. What happened next startled me back to the present.

There was a loud shout from the surrounding bushes, followed by the calling of men's voices. Through the trees I could see moving figures appearing and disappearing as they came closer. Suddenly the men burst out into the open and ran on to the prepared ground. They were wearing only trousers, and their upper bodies were painted with several different designs in white, red, and black. They wore leaves or feathers in their headband *yakirris*, and carried small branches from eucalyptus trees in each hand. Several men from the perimeter arose and joined them, yet remained at a short distance from them. There followed what I would describe as a dance, although I had seen nothing like it before, only pictures in anthropology books. No doubt there was some significance to the postures and actions, but I was completely captured by the emotional impact, and was not able to guess the symbolism.

Silence returned as the dancing ceased, with all the characters assuming various postures. Some knelt, some stood upright, some sat, some bent over, and one lay on the ground. After a moment they relaxed and took their places with their families. Four men now approached the grave. Two carefully stepped into the open hole while the other two took the head and feet of the body and carried it very gently and reverently to the grave. The four then laid the body in the bed of leaves, while those watching began wailing in loud continuous cries. It took several minutes for the men to be satisfied that the body was positioned correctly, and they climbed out of the open pit.

I expected them to begin shoveling the soil into the grave, but instead they walked to the perimeter, where I noticed for the first time a number of long branches about two inches thick. They carried them back to the grave and placed them lengthwise over the top as a covering to prevent dogs or dingoes from getting to the body. Evidently they would not completely bury the body at this time, and I remembered yesterday evening's discussion; that it takes about nine months for the body to disintegrate sufficiently for the spirit to not recognize it as his any longer, and thus be ready finally to make the next move to *Tjukurrpa*.

The ceremony was finished. People began to silently walk away toward the mission and on to their camp. Today they would be moving to a new site. There was work to be done. Toby, and his wife Evelyn carrying their child, came over to our small non-Aboriginal group and hugged us all, including my four children. Nothing was said at first, but then Toby spoke to me and Bill, asking, "Junnerstan' what you bin seein'?"

"I think so," I responded, "but this is the first *Wangkayi* funeral I've seen, and it's different from what I'm used to." I hesitated to spoil the impact by asking for explanations.

However, Toby earnestly looked into our eyes and said, "We can't put 'im back in his mother's belly, so we put 'im back in the earth womb ready to set 'im free. He gets born again, an' we help 'im when we bin finish the funeral nex' year."

"I like the idea of burying him in a blanket," I said.

Toby turned to Bill and reminded him of his first funeral at Cundeelee. "You made a wooden box, 'member? We didn' like that. People who get born on the groun', live on the groun', sleep on the ground, get groun' all over 'em, doan' want to be put in a box for their las' sleep."

"I remember," Bill responded. "You also told us that our houses were like coffins. Like boxes for the dead, you said. We put ourselves into smaller coffin rooms inside, and shut the lids, and don't sit close, or sleep close like you do. You all find a place near the fire and near each other. There's a lesson there." Bill laughed. "I haven't learned the lesson yet. I still build the coffin houses." They all joined in with laughter.

Toby's comments are worth reflecting on: 'Lemme tell you something. You can't grow inside a box with a lid on it. That like a coffin box . . . made for death. You gotta push open the lid an' look aroun'. That the way you learn'."

The simple but profound wisdom of this metaphor was not lost to me. I was awakening to the reality that I was living in a box, indeed several boxes, my culture and language, my religion, my prejudices, my judgments of what was right and wrong, my world views, and so much more.

My mind had been trapped in these boxes, but the lids were opening one by one, revealing interesting and challenging possibilities. I was tentatively intrigued by what potentials lay there, and my mind began to grasp what investigating and accepting new thought processes would mean to others in my boxes. They would be threatened, would judge me in their terms, and either set out to woo me back, or to reject me as a heretic. All of this because I was beginning to appreciate another culture. The one I had come to Cundeelee to change.

As Bill and I drove with the children back to the mission in the Jeep, each one kept silence with his own thoughts.

It was almost 10 o'clock when I rang the school bell. I was not surprised to see Wally marching over to the school building. Without any preliminaries he announced, "A bit late to start school for the day, isn't it?"

To avoid a confrontation, I did not reply. This annoyed Wally who curtly stated, "The Education Department will hear of this." Wally turned and walked away, leaving me puzzled but not intimidated by the threat.

There was a special subdued tone in the school that morning, no doubt the result of the funeral, but as the day wore on the children's usual exuberance returned.

I have never forgotten that experience. It penetrated deeply into my being, transforming my thinking and my behavior. I was beginning to realize the importance of being more consciously aware about what I was doing, the choices I made, the available boxes, the ones I created, and the relationships between them.

Thoughts about my freedom to choose, and the abrogation of responsibility by maintaining obedience to the church's requirements filtered into my mind. Was I really trying to please God or Jesus, or was I a slave to their demands on my allegiance? If I was the obedient slave, then these others must accept the responsibility for my decisions and actions. Their 'thou shalts or shalt nots' would be my way out, my excuses.

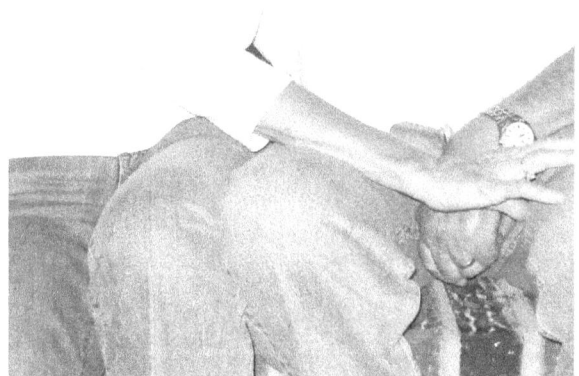

GAYLE AND ROBERT
McKEICH—2008

Chapter Five

MARRIAGE 101

My first marriage of 30 years was with Betty, made in wartime, for the security and love desired by a young man in the army. As was the custom then, Betty did not work outside our home, and cared well for our four children. She was a willing partner when we migrated to Australia to establish the Aboriginal Mission School at Cundeelee. For several years Betty and I worked at the Katukutu Hostel for Aboriginal young men that we pioneered in Perth. She supported my studies at the University of Western Australia, and my several teaching positions in Primary and Secondary schools, and Universities.

However, as I considered and responded to the influence of the Aborigines, and matured in my studies, Betty felt left behind, declaring that she preferred to remain in her church box where she felt safe. Living together became difficult and uncomfortable so we divorced.

It was because of my education, ultimately with a PhD, that Betty and I travelled from Perth to Shawnee, Oklahoma in an exchange program for me to teach at the Oklahoma Baptist University for one and a half years. Among the courses I taught was Marriage and Family, one I had never encountered before. It was a most interesting and thoughtful introduction that challenged and awakened my thoughts on marriage, especially my marriage. One of my students was Gayle Mills, with whom I eventually felt comfortable to discuss private thoughts, and who was comfortable with me. Our growing relationship is expressed in fairy tale form in the next chapter.

The transition from one marriage to another was most difficult. Let no one tell you that divorce is the easy way out. First there were the uncertainties of ending the relationship, questions about validating the reasons for the move, and the processes of disengagement. People who knew little of my changing perspective made judgments and took sides. I felt very alone. I made an encouraging and peaceful attachment to a woman named Kathleen in Perth for a year, but my thoughts constantly returned to Gayle in Oklahoma, who was experiencing her own divorce. Eventually she flew to Australia where we spent many hours developing our new relationship. We have been together since 1976.

The nature of Marriage

Traditionally, we take for granted the meanings and expectations of marriage, much of our knowledge being based on that of our experiences with parents or parent substitutes. Adolescent peers add another dimension to our knowledge and expectations. Choosing a partner, linking up, and getting married also involves a whole range of variables such as ethnic or race characteristics, cultural and sub-cultural backgrounds, age, religion, social status, education, sexual orientation, and most significantly who and where we meet.

For some the wedding is more significant than the marriage. I make a distinction here. Marriage is the special kind of relationship between the couple, while the wedding is the instrument by which getting married is publicly declared, legitimated, and sanctioned by law and very often the religious system. If you think about it, you do not have a wedding to get married, you are already married or you would not choose to have a wedding.

Many people are not ready for marriage. They plan and perform the wedding, but risk the marriage. More thought and energy goes into the preparations for the wedding than into the lifetime commitment. In his book *The Power Of Myth*, Joseph Campbell wrote, "But marriage is marriage, you know. Marriage is not a love affair. A love affair is a totally different thing. A marriage is a commitment to that which you are. That person is literally your other half. And you and the other are one. A love affair isn't that. That is a relationship for pleasure, and when it gets to be unpleasurable, it's off. But a marriage is a life commitment, and a life commitment means the prime concern of your life. If marriage is not the prime concern, you're not married."

Romance

Then there's romance. Ideas of what is romantic are numerous and varied. The range of possibilities is infinite. Romantic thoughts and expressions change over the years, and in a particular relationship may diminish after the first year or so. How can you maintain the romance? Should we?

I think so. By continuing to court, we maintain romance throughout our marriage. We recognize the changes in what is regarded as romantic as we face life changes, but there is no doubt that basic romantic attraction can be maintained and even enhanced. I write love poems to Gayle, which are reminders to her of our relationship, and also reminders to me about how I perceive her. Here's one I wrote for her 67th birthday:

MY FUNNY WOMAN

What magic do you weave into my heart?
Why do you affect me so – and how?

Long years ago when I first felt it start,
I did not understand it then – or now.

Since you roamed with me upon life's winding trail,
I walk with lighter steps and happier days,
I puzzled on your tricks to no avail,
And just accept these samples of your ways.

You give me cause to smile from time to time,
A natural act, I cannot help my inner joy,
You are there to tease, the pleasure's mine,
And I wonder at the wiles that you employ.

You come home late, your face I see,
I laugh to know you really meant,
Those Post-it love note words on my PC,
And all the love throughout the day you sent.

We walk the trails together in the sun,
We share our tasks, the shopping, and the car,
We cuddle into bed, spooned close as one,
My funny woman in my heart is what you are.

No magic, wiles, or other artificial tricks are there concealed,
You generate your wholesome spirit, truly human,
I find it's simply you, yourself that is revealed,
You are indeed my own, my special funny woman.

Gayle attaches Post-it notes to my computer monitor and keyboard where I discover them. These 'post-it love notes' are devices, gimmicks if you like, but gimmicks with a deep intent. Ways of saying, "I love you." They are a form of nurturing.

Here are a couple of samples:
My Rob, You are the sunshine of my life, even when the sun
doesn't shine! ! Know I Love You! ! ! G

Rob, Our Love for each other is what makes our world go around. My precious man, Let my caring thoughts of and for you be ever-present in your mind, and know that I'm always near you! Yours, G

I have 500 of these notes.

One of my own romantic gestures is to be the Quarter Fairy who delivers quarters (25 cent coins) into Gayle's shoes, shirt pockets, on lotion caps, taped to her computer mouse and cover, under her dinner plate, under the clothes iron, and other unusual places. We both know that these are games, especially with the elusive, invisible Quarter Fairy, but the pretense is part of the romance. I receive a "Thank you" kiss for each quarter found.

Respect

I recognize that the term 'Funny Woman' in the poem could be either derogatory or a term of affection. I needed to be careful when I wrote it so that I could send a message of respect not criticism. Any relationship needs to be carefully nurtured, and that's done through the very basic technique of 'respect'. Indeed, 'respect' is the foundation of all positive social interaction. Respect for others breeds respect for oneself. It is a gentle and very strong way of seeing and appreciating others as real people with real qualities. To see them as a total person, not just a stereotype, a category, a class.

It is something that one needs to consciously practice in a marriage – lose respect and the marriage is in trouble. It's not very difficult to cultivate.

Love and appreciate

I have a definition of love, one of many, but I frequently, almost every day remind myself of its significance: "The enhancement of the self through the enhancement of the other." Respect, support and encouragement, are a constant reinforcement of the other's qualities. When I appreciate

Gayle she feels as if she is important to me and is enhanced. I am also uplifted by her pleasurable response and am happy that I communicated my appreciation. If I should put her down, I am doing the same thing to myself. In his book *You'll See It When You Believe It*, Wayne Dyer wrote the truth about judgment: "When you are strongly attached to judging anyone, you are not defining him or her, you are defining yourself."

Marriage is a very precarious relationship that ideally begins with love and the respect that goes with it. Two very different people form a partnership that has the potential for bliss or conflict. One can overlook or romanticize the 'faults', or address them in a mature respectful way.

Remember we are dealing with a complex and very intimate relationship. It need not be a chore to maintain such a wonderful mutually sustaining situation, but it needs thought and creativity for its fulfillment.

Most people take their world for granted without questioning or analyzing their place within it. They take care of the practicalities of the marriage, children, establishing a home, employment and income, health and more, but scarcely consider the nature and underpinnings of their relationship.

With Gayle and me it's a two-way thing, involving both of us, and it works on two levels. First, we think about the concept of marriage, a philosophy of marriage if you wish, a set of principles, and not merely the individual self-centered practice of our own marriage. We ask what does it mean for me to be married to someone who agrees to share their life? Then we realize that our marriage is a dynamic, creative attitude, with a rational philosophy for life, whether associated with the transcendental or not . . . whether the love is seen as a gift from God, or a manifestation of what is good within our own being.

Second, it's a conscious determination to take action in the real world, in the 'being married' realm. It is important to answer the question: How do I conduct my marriage? Life doesn't just happen. We need to be involved, to take charge, to accept responsibility, and not rely on others whether they are people or 'gods', for decisions that ought to be ours. These thoughts go way beyond marriage into every fabric of our lives.

Human personalities are involved as much as the belief systems. We are all unique and come together to share that uniqueness in a marriage. Some individuals may want to dominate while others are willing to be dominated by the other, or by a parent, or even by the requirements of their faith. This can be positively reinforcing to the relationship, or at the other extreme quite destructive.

A partnership

In a modern western style marriage, where the economic foundation has largely changed from rural and traditional industrial, and where women have more equal 'rights', sharing roles is becoming the norm, especially where both partners are employed. Gayle works full time and has defined her role in the kitchen so to speak, but we have both always shared the kitchen activities right from the beginning, and she also shared the creation and shaping of my work, editing, making suggestions, debriefing following speeches, adding ideas that did not come to my mind, encouraging me when things got difficult. We always shared major decisions, and together prepared for our travels. A partnership you might say.

There will be tremendous variations between families but an awareness of the open role possibilities can mean the difference between a happy relationship and a miserable one.

The trap of expectations and control

The trap seems to be that one partner lays down expectations for the other partner. When these expectations are not met there may be conflict, especially when the expectations are not verbalized. Of course there must be expectations in human society or we could not continue to function. From birth we are taught and encounter expected behavior. That is what makes us safe. However, in a marriage one member may try to control the other by being demanding or by manipulating the other. It's a delicate balance between what is reasonable and what may be dictatorial or abusive.

Viva la difference! – and how to navigate it
It is the differences that brought Gayle and me together as much as the similarities. We allow for the differences and treasure them. Once they may have been part of the romance and with an open mind they may continue to be so.
Let me summarize some of the techniques for dealing with differences in thoughts and behavior that might cause trouble. Remember they are only a few of the many possibilities.

1.Basic to all relationship is respect. Lose respect and you have lost the relationship and the argument.
2. Listen – listen – listen. Ask and listen. Don't interrupt, no matter how tempting that might be. Do not both talk at the same time. Do not over talk the other person. Agree to take turns and wait for your turn. Listen – listen - listen when the other is speaking.
3. Avoid shouting at each other.

Personal responsibility
Along with respect, responsibility is one of our major life themes. When I was younger, and that's a long time ago, I would habitually put the responsibility for my choices and behavior on others. I blamed my parents, siblings, teachers, friends, and circumstances, even lying about what happened. Partly that was in fear of punishment, but it was also the attitude my father had adopted and communicated to us children – but that is another story. That continued when I adopted a religious dimension to my life. I put the

responsibility on Jesus and God. They chose my behavior, my choices, my reasons for acting the way I did, my sources for judgment and approval. This was a cop-out. In my early thirties, among the Aborigines and in my studies, I woke up to see that the way I perceived myself in the world was diminishing my freedom. I was accepting a slave mentality with the Lord being my Master, my boss, my controlling influence, my cop-out from taking responsibility for my life. Peter Berger, a sociologist, called it 'bad faith'. I began to see how this put me in a box, inhibited my freedom, stifled my creativity, and reduced my world. I was constantly fearful that I might displease someone and receive punishment. When I began to admit my responsibility for my actions I was immediately liberated from a life that relied on others, even God, for justification. I was free.

When you take responsibility for your life you stop making excuses. You carefully assess your judgments, you do not assign blame or say, "It's your fault". Thoughtfully and consciously ask if what you are saying are really 'excuses'. I worked this out some time ago and have used it in guiding people. It's about responsibility.

1. You have a problem or a number of problems
2. Basically the problem is yours, not mine, or anyone else's
3. The problem has arisen, in the ultimate analysis, because of your choices, or because of circumstances outside those choices, but nevertheless related to them
4. You must accept the responsibility
   (a) for making those choices, or being in those circumstances
   (b) for holding onto those choices
   (c) for the results of those choices
   (d) for seeking out the solutions to the problems brought about by those choices
5. You cannot ignore or run away from the problems, nor can

you expect others to take the responsibility for providing the solutions to those problems

6. You must look for creative and positive ways

    (a) of dealing with the immediate problems

    (b) of dealing with long-range problems

    (c) of avoiding, or dealing with problems in the future

7. You may ask for help in solving the problems, but

    (a) they must be your solutions

    (b) the help must be directed to helping you to solve the problems rather than others taking over for you

8. If there are others involved in the problems, they must be encouraged to share in the process

    (a) of problem awareness

    (b) of developing resolution strategies

    (c) of disciplines required for pursuing the strategies of resolution

9. The strategies and solutions must be reasonable, achievable, responsible, and positive. Their success or failure depends on you, so no-one else may be blamed or accused if they do not achieve their goals

10. Recognize that problems are not necessarily negative or destructive, but are the means by which you may grow to maturity, exercise your creative abilities, demonstrate your independence, draw from and give love, increase your security, take responsibility for your life, and ultimately achieve those goals, both human and material, that are important to you.

No room for "Poor me", blaming, or dependency; just taking responsibility for one's life.

Disagreement

Right. There will always be differences of information, opinion and perspective and indeed disagreements are expected and not necessarily negative. How you argue is most important, and what you choose to argue about can make the difference between problem solving and generating major tensions.

An argument is not just an argument, it is not merely a matter of solving problems and releasing emotions, it is a way to express and cement a whole range of social relationships. You only argue with certain people who are associated with you in some way. Arguments have a dynamic of their own. Ideally arguments have their own 'rules of the game'. Too frequently the rules are broken with devastating consequences to the marriage.

Here is a list of do's and don'ts in discussions – I prefer 'discussion' to 'argument'.

- Note if you are keeping to the topic. Watch out for the introduction of side issues.
- Know the difference between dealing with feelings versus objective issues – although objective issues may involve passion, commitment, emotions.
- Beware of prejudices, lying, shouting, and ignorance. Always tell the truth as you see it, and be willing to consider another truth
- Watch out for the diversion from discussing the real object and intent of the discussion, and the side tracking on to blaming, or name calling.
- Remember that winning the argument does not necessarily solve the problem. Each person must exit with dignity.
- The topic and mood can quickly change when one needs to defend their position or deny emotions imputed by one of the parties.
- Never say, "I know what you are thinking." This raises a totally different side issue from the topic under discussion, to whether you are right or wrong about what they are thinking. Always ask, "Tell me what you are thinking."
- If the matter can be solved by a measurement, searching the atlas or dictionary, or the Internet, do so.

Recognize opinions and speculation, versus the reality
• Agree to stop and move on when discussion is completed or turns to a fruitless activity.
• Have a cup of tea. A hot cuppa can do wonders.
Remember that these are not 'Thou shalts' or 'Thou shalt nots' but merely guidelines for effective communication. Now, where's that cuppa?

Sex

A word about sex. Intercourse is a simple and universal phenomena, but it is also a most complicated and difficult biological, moral, ethical, religious, social, legal, psychological, health and personal matter in human life.

We begin learning from the moment we are born, or before. The big gender question, 'is the baby a boy or a girl?' begins a life direction for the child, including a set of relationships leading to the sexual experiences. Society has the 'rules' already established; growing up implants most of them. Very soon we know what is 'naughty' and what is 'nice'.

Now we come back to our basic themes. First of all, having sex ought to include the utmost in respect, each person for the other. That may include abstinence. To claim that you are in love is not a sufficient reason on its own. Secondly, there is a tremendous responsibility involved. In my younger days pregnancy was the potential that we wanted to avoid, especially outside the marriage. Nowadays it is STIs that are the risk. While there are birth control methods available, and condoms, there is the challenge of responsibility, to use them responsibly when necessary. Responsibility goes beyond pregnancy and disease, to the meaning in religious, ethical, legal areas, plus possible exploitation, and support if there should be children.

One more thing, the 'sexual drive' it's called, changes over time and according to life circumstances. In the earlier years of a relationship, making love can be a most satisfying expression of mutual love. But a deep and whole intimate relationship grows beyond sex. There is a transition period in which making love takes on a deeper meaning. The deeper meaning then becomes the source of the relationship, and a oneness develops that is beyond the dichotomy of man/woman. Eventually, later in life, health, ageing, hormones, and many other reasons may reduce the sex drive. In these later stages of our lives the love, respect and responsibility Gayle and I share is more significant than making physical love. We love now in a different manner, and because we nurtured our physical love when younger, we are enhanced by a different but no less real kind of love.

Joseph Campbell wrote: "Love itself is a pain, you might say – the pain of being truly alive." This poem tells of the depth of love and the pain of loss. In it, I consider the effect of 'losing' the physical form called Gayle. I wrote it to express how I see the being that is Gayle, and the nature of our love.

ONESOUL

For if this form shall evermore be lost,
Her frame shall fade, but spirit linger on,
The body frail shall turn to dust,
And in the earth shall lie,
The memories of time, and place, and space,
Shall be the blessings which linger in this world.
They build anew the joy and peace and love,
Yet add the pain of treasures won and gone.
But now forever, the memories remain
To fill the days with light,
But in the darkness of the night
They draw the tears of grief.
No more to touch the skin so smooth and soft,

The voice forever hushed,
Hair nevermore to lie caressed by wind.
And, however warm the love was in the past,
A one way love now dominates the scene,
With desires unfulfilled.
Now to live alone in that remorseful mood,
Yet not alone, for she lives on in me.
The touch imprinted in my fingertips,
The voice still sweet and low within my ears,
A vision dimly clear my mind recalls,
And with it joy which lasts throughout the years.
We merged in life, our two souls grew as one,
And that remains though one of us is gone.
The two made one,
Not each, but both endure.
What once was shared, filled full our heart's
desire,
And what was reached in passion,
The fruit of mutual trust,
Drawing, weaving, molding, satisfying,
Found contentment in the best of lust.
The dreams fulfilled, and those which stayed as
dreams,
To court our hopes and plans,
We found in our imaginings,
The richness and completeness of our open minds.
Oh joy supreme, we lived and lived again,
In bonded lives, where joy exceeds the pain.
But now the pain remains, a new and treasured
thing.
The pain of having loved and shared and grown,
In ways which measure cannot tell.

1979 SEPT FLORENCE ITALY
ROB GAYLE PASTEL PORTRAIT

Chapter Six

ONCE UPON A TIME

People often ask how Gayle and I met and 'hooked up'. She is an American from Oklahoma, and I am a Kiwi/ Australian. Many big adventures begin with small events. In 1969, I was teaching Sociology and Anthropology at the Western Australian Institute of Technology (now known as the Curtin University) when I was approached by Noel Vose, the Principal of the Baptist College. He had a brief letter from Professor Doug Clark at the Oklahoma Baptist University inquiring about the possibility of a temporary teaching position while he was on a sabbatical. The Baptist College did not have an opening, but Noel thought WAIT might have one. We did not have a position but after some thought Doug and I arranged an exchange of jobs, houses, and cars. That simple handwritten note changed my life academically and personally.

This is a true story, and yet it is a kind of fairy tale. I call it

RABBIT AND THE TEACHER.
"ONCE UPON A TIME there lived a beautiful princess.
Her face was attractive and serene; her eyes sharp and shining; her smile as the waking of the dawn; her ears so sensitive that when the breeze blew upon them she shivered

69

with delight and fell helpless on the ground. Wind loved to make her do this. Wind also loved to caress the long brown hair that cascaded to her waist. She was swift as a deer, and like a fish she swam in the nearby lakes, rivers, and pools. She imagined she could fly like Hawk to faraway places, to swim in the great ocean that the elders spoke about, to communicate with Deer, Bear, Horse, and Bison. She was happy in her teepee among the Shawnee, playing her childhood games in the open plains. Her name was "Rabbit with the Heart of a Cougar".

Learning from her strong mother was not easy. Her mother demanded instant obedience, making her clean the family teepee, work long hours fetching firewood and food, and cooking in the fashion of her tribe; but that prepared her for life as a grown woman. She was very happy. In due time, as she matured, she longed for a companion, a man who could hold and love her and give her children to complete a family.

One day, while wandering near the still waters, she spied a handsome brave from Wisconsin. He was gentle and kind, small yet strong, not a warrior. "This is my man," she thought, "the one I have waited and looked for, the one who will fulfill my dreams of love and companionship, the one who will share my teepee, the one with whom I may grow, the one who will create great adventures, and give me strong children."

In due time they performed the wedding rituals in the sacred meeting house. Four children came to them, and she thought they would all live happily ever after among her Shawnee people.

Although she seemed to have everything a woman could want she was not entirely happy. She walked with grace upon the earth, and reveled in the love of her family; she actively filled

70

her days with work and brought sunshine to all around her, but felt as if her life was bound, stifled, incomplete. The love she first experienced no longer sustained her. It diminished and grew cool for want of reciprocation, because her man spent many hours in isolation, and rarely showed affection. Gradually Rabbit lost the desire to fly like Hawk, or swim the great ocean. Bear, Deer, Horse, and Bison noticed her withdrawing, and began to worry about her. She was no more fun.

She was as a bird in a cage, with stunted and useless wings, ready to fly but without strength. She longed for more, but was not sure what that could be. Perhaps she should be content to live in the poverty of her yearning heart. Sadness, yes, but no bitterness entered her soul. She was not like that. Only a few of her close friends knew of the depths of longing in her Cougar Heart.

One cold winter night around the campfire, while celebrating a change of seasons, she noticed a dusky warrior from a faraway tribe in the south, truly a redskin, not pale like her people. He had traveled across the great ocean, a medicine man, a teacher in the great meeting tents. His wise words spoke of adventure, of excitement, of communication with the true spirits of life. He knew much of other tribes and respected them all, and he did not boast or talk down to his listeners. Days later she sat at his feet, drinking his words and asking the questions that had troubled her heart and mind, questions of the meaning of life, of the great spirits, of love. The Teacher listened with respect, beginning to discern the longing implied in her earnest conversation.

Her dulling eyes began to sparkle once more. Wind stirred her ears, gently thrusting her smiling to the ground. Her long hair shone again. Earth felt her eager dancing steps, and Water sensuously enveloped her in the pools, Bison

71

winked an eye, and Hawk beckoned her to fly. Others of her tribe also found time to gather at the Teacher's feet, or wandered with him into the forests.

A different kind of love entered Rabbit's being, and passions awakened to disturb in the most delightful way. His spell affected her like that in an ancient fairy tale. Within the joy, caution warned her of a price that might be demanded should she allow the spell to overcome her wisdom. The compulsion of love could not be denied or resisted; it controlled her, and yet she knew that she must be in control. Whatever happened must be her own choice. The Teacher had said that about all things. Was he immune to the beauty of this woman named Rabbit with the Heart of a Cougar? Did he find love in her? For now that did not matter, she was drinking of the Water of Love.

Time became lost in his presence, and she wanted more and more to be with him. But Time was also an enemy, for Time would soon be taking him away, back to his southern land where all was upside down, where seasons were reversed, the sun moved northwards across the sky, snow was never seen, and some animals bounded around like dancing children. A door to her soul had opened and Rabbit wanted to walk through it, to be with her Teacher. But perhaps the Teacher had opened the door for her to walk alone?

In his way her husband had loved her, she was responsible for their children, and her tribal family would not understand. How could she abandon them for a growing love that also would not abandon her, and perhaps only had a sorrowful destiny? Did this new Teacher love her? She could not be sure of that. Should she try to keep him here? Would he let her travel away with him? Her mind was troubled. Perhaps the easiest path would be to let him go away and settle for the best she could make of life with the Shawnee.

The Teacher would need to make his own decisions.

One day, alone together in a large canoe, she declared her love to him. Teacher responded with encouragement, and in his wisdom said he deeply loved Rabbit with the Heart of a Cougar. He cautioned that whatever happened should be the best for them both. For the present, they could not be together. He warned her again that he must soon leave to return to his own tribe and perhaps she would forget him. The Teacher left one day, suddenly, as if he had taken flight.

Years passed. She grew pale, her body wasting with longing. Tears were not far from her once sparkling eyes. While caring for her husband and children, while moving around the camp, while cooking and cleaning in her teepee, the Teacher was always in her mind.

Now she faced the agony of decision. Rabbit tried to be faithful to her family commitments, but was yet obsessed with the departed Teacher. Would the gain of being with him be worth the loss of leaving the Shawnee? Venturing into the unknown south could be a nightmare, and not the imagined dream. She could not decide. She had to know if this was fairy tale real with a happy ending, or real real with pain, sorrow, and perhaps even death. She took counsel from some elders and her close friends with mixed advice. Why leave the status quo for an unknown dream they asked? In taking the risk she might lose both what she had, and her dream life with the Teacher.

Her mind and heart could not rest. She wandered the village and trails as in two worlds. Her Shawnee people grew concerned and warned her of dire results to her mental health if she did not climb back into the comfort zone of their box. All she needed they said could be found in this camp. Her dilemma did not diminish. The love she carried built courage within, and to be with the absent Teacher continued to be a goal she must achieve. Message sticks passed between them carried by huge migrating birds. Words of encouragement from the Teacher who also struggled with his emotions and the circumstances of their intertwining lives gave Rabbit hope. Her heart began to soar. At last she was beginning to believe she could satisfy her longings, and with a tentative start she flew like Hawk across the great ocean into the Teacher's welcoming arms. Joy was fulfilled, a new life awakened.

For many years they roamed the world, met people from other tribes, walked barefoot in the deserts, climbed mountains, swam naked in many waters, and shared their love with others. She returned to the Shawnee on many occasions, and took her growing children on treks into nature, or shared the quietness of their homes, helping them to grow strong and independent.

Their love grew beyond measure, and THEY BOTH LIVED HAPPILY EVER AFTER."

* * * * * *

That is the end of the fairy tale, as it should be, rooted in the metaphors of reality. But our marriage is more than a fairy tale. The meeting and the getting together parts were easy, despite the distance and uncertainties. Many years of living, laughing, and loving, nurtured by respect and sensitivity, have created bonds that seem to transcend ordinary living.

Love has matured over time, and an intimacy of our minds has grown into a oneness that seems miraculous. Gayle and I are two quite different individuals, but are united in this marriage relationship. There is so much that enhances our togetherness that differences are welcomed as ways of growing. We teach and learn from each other. There is no sense of controlling. Both of us have freedom to pursue our individual interests, and yet have developed this partnership. We try to be sensitive to the qualities and needs of the other. No put downs, or one upmanship, just loving acceptance. We have no secrets from each other, only our own mutual ones. There are no jealousies to mar our relationship.

"What is it then, in a nutshell, that contributes to your harmony?" Several things come to mind. Love tokens such as the post-it love notes, and the Quarter Fairy games add romance and fun to the ordinary world. Tender touching, gentle warm hugs, and lingering kisses do not go astray. The words, "Thank you.", and most importantly, "I love you" enhance our pleasure.

GAYLE, ERIC, ROBERT & ROBERT
SETTING OUT ON BICYCLE TOUR
THROUGH EUROPE, 1979

Chapter Seven

FIJI AND FRANCE

66Always walk the Straight and Narrow." That's what
my parents said, as did my teachers, and the church.
Good advice? Not "Always". You may feel safe, keep out
of trouble and achieve your goals. However, you may also
miss so much that is new and exciting.

These two adventures actually began in Perth where Gayle
and I bought plane tickets to Los Angeles for a Sabbatical in
Minneapolis on a study program in Death and Dying with
Robert Fulton. As we were to travel all that distance, we
decided to stop off in the Pacific. After much discussion
with our travel agent, we arranged for stopovers at Sydney,
Auckland, Fiji, Oahu and big island of Hawaii. The agent
informed us that we had some travel miles left over, so we
added Western Samoa and Molokai. She then said we had
85 miles left on our tickets. We asked her to find us an
island and she pointed out Tongatapu, plus we would need
to fly from Western Samoa to American Samoa in order to
reach Hawaii. The phrase, "Find us an island" has been part
of our travel repertoire ever since.

On Fiji, in Suva, Gayle and I, together with her sons Eric and
Robert, rented a car. We set out to circumnavigate the island
of Viti Levu with a fire walking demonstration at Lautoka in

mind. On my previous visit I had seen only the wet eastern side of the island, with its tall trees and lush vegetation, but this time we investigated the dry western side. About 30 miles from Suva I had the impulse to see the coast. "Let's take the next road to the right!" I declared. That's what we did, driving a dusty, winding road of 23 miles, with old fence posts sprouting new growth. There must be a message in that.

The road ended at the sea shore, where an isolated village was established. On a nearby hill was the village school. We stopped by a shallow creek with an ancient looking wooden bridge. It was our custom to ask permission from the headman to enter such villages but there was no one around to ask. We took out our lunch, cheese and fresh bread, and with our Swiss army knives began to share. Shortly, children from the school marched by, looking fresh and orderly in their school uniforms. Although the children were shy, the teacher came over to talk, and to welcome us to her village. No tourists ever visited here.

While we ate, we were entertained by the children shyly walking down the hill from the school to look at us, and then scurrying away laughing when we waved to them. That was fun for us all. And then, down the road came possible trouble. Shouting at us, and pointing back up the road we had driven, strode a man saying something in Fijian. Our immediate interpretation was that he was displeased with our intrusion and he wanted us to leave. Not willing to give offence we began to pack up and climb into the car. I waited for him to come close in order to apologize, but he moved in quickly to grab my arm, still speaking Fijian and gesticulating back up the road. There were several minutes of non-communication, or rather mis-communication.

Suddenly the teacher was there. She spoke to the man and then to us. "He is inviting you to his home to drink kava." I knew about kava, the ritual and symbolic nature of the ceremonies, and the great honor he was showing us. We could not refuse.

Seated on mats on the floor we gazed around. As honored guests we had been invited to sit on the worn and tired couch, but when I indicated we would like to sit on the floor as they did, they were immediately pleased. While the old man prepared the kava root in a large wooden kava bowl, we communicated as best we could with hand signals and body language. I was happy to note that they were not totally traditional in their preparation by chewing the kava root and spitting it into the bowl to ferment. They used water. As the oldest guest I was honored with the first drink, and was taught the correct hand clapping and declarations of satisfaction. Our family joined in drinking with them, and even though we did not find the taste as attractive as Coke, we knew that this new experience was more than merely satisfying our thirst. The teacher joined us after about an hour, interpreting to add communication. It turned out to be a very exciting and satisfying event.

The family invited us to spend the night with them, and were genuinely disappointed when we said we needed to continue on for the fire walking on the other side of the island. They gave us gifts of food and a grass mat. The "next road to the right" had been something special.

The other experience arose from a error . Well, it began as an error, but we have never interpreted it as something we did wrong. Perhaps 'mistakes' are not mistakes after all. It is what you do with your mistake, how you interpret it.

 Once again we left the 'straight and narrow'. In France, on our way back home from Minneapolis to Perth, we were in our tiny Morris Minor van with bicycles on top, six of us, Gayle and me, her three adolescent boys and a friend. Somehow we took a wrong turning. Not 'wrong' in a judgmental sense, but not the one we intended. It's a matter of the 'definition of the situation'.

As on our way north from Australia the year before, we planned to maximize our time and our creative minds on our way south. We were somewhat ambitious in choosing to bicycle through Great Britain, France, Netherlands, Brussels, Germany, Austria, Switzerland, Italy, Greece, Israel, and possibly India. (Now India was something entirely different. We never actually travelled in India, but had a wonderful adventure there.)

Back to France. Somehow we misread the map, or the road signs, and found ourselves on a narrow country road. Too late to turn back. We never booked ahead on this journey, but took our chances at finding a campground for the night when it began to grow dark, so a change in our plans did not matter too much. We had gone about fifteen miles when a policeman emerged from the side of the road and motioned us to pull over and park. He then turned his back on us and walked up the hill. Evidently he was not going to arrest us . . . but what lay over the hill?

We had driven into a local Saint's Day or harvest festival in the village of Cerilly. The parade was in full swing, with a statue of the village saint being carried on the shoulders of six men, a band, marching girls dressed in very short skirts, floats with agricultural themes, and vendors selling homemade candy, cakes, and cookies, fruits and vegetables. This was not prepared for tourists, but for themselves. Pride and bonhomie were evident. It was a village celebration, simple yet profound in its communal expression. But, the short skirted marching girls . . . they really caught my attention.

That night, from our campground in a paddock in another village, we could hear sounds of happy talking, and music from a hurdy gurdy. Evidently another celebration was in progress. To this day I wished I had generated the courage to walk over and visit. I know we would have been welcomed and invited to join them.

Where do you want to go? Not only in your travels but in your life's journey? On a tour bus style guided journey through life, associated only with those of a like mind, shepherded from place to place, shielded from alien contact, slaves to the predetermined itinerary, or, are you free to choose this road or that, and free to change your route as you go?

Have the courage to dare to be different, as the McKeich clan motto states *Dhandeon co Heiragha*, "Despite Who Would Gainsay". Have a go, do what you feel with no regrets. Take chances, the mistakes you make are opportunities, doors to unexpected experiences.

Live in the now. There is an infinite number of "nows" each a onetime gift to make your life count. The wisdom of the Aborigines slowly entered my life to create a special understanding of my inner being, and to transform my ways of living. These thoughts were reinforced by my studies, by encounters with interesting people, and by stepping into many adventures.

The "straight and narrow" is OK, but fun and adventure are also found on the "next road to the right".

ROBERT TEACHING ANTHROPOLOGY
STUDENTS

AT THE UNIVERSITY OF WISCONSIN

EAU CLAIRE, 1987

Chapter Eight

DIRT FROM OUR EARS, MUD FROM OUR EYES

How can I sew this up into one bag, the anecdotes, adventures, philosophies, and awakenings? Is it possible to express in a few words the measure of my life? Aubrey, I wrote this for you, and for anyone who chooses to listen. I, your Great Granddad Robert, have many memories to call upon, but you, Aubrey are just beginning to create your own. I strongly wish that some of what I have hinted at here might become part of your own experiences, in your own unique way.

I am at peace with the world, others, and myself, and view my life positively, no regrets, no guilt. I do not judge myself, I try to not judge others, and am not unduly concerned with the judgments of others. Of course I have conformed to social and cultural norms, one must do that or be labeled an eccentric, criminal, heretic, deviant, or 'strange', but within the range of acceptable behavior, I have been able to be a Master of my soul. I try to avoid the existential Slave mentality, as well as the concepts of blame and failure. There is a difference between variation within the social norms or deviation from the norms. In variation you remain within the range of norms, in deviation you move outside socially acceptable boundaries. I am a 'variant'.

Love, joy, peace, and bliss, are not mere words. I have lived those, making conscious choices to not become embroiled in failure, blame, hatred, anger, domination, manipulation, one upmanship, put downs, and disrespect.

I am imbued with a mountain of curiosity. I love to listen, observe, read, travel, taste and ask questions, to have an open mind. There are those who for personal reasons say, "I don't want to know". But, "I do want to know".

I love beach walking and spending time 'in the bush'. This poem expresses my emotions both for the bush and for Gayle.

THOUGHTS ABOUT GAYLE IN THE SUNSET AT CUNDEELEE

Sunset on the clouds,
Reflections on the desert sea,
Bird wings catching light,
Falling leaves in fairy dances flying.
Living, changing palettes of this world.
I do not try to comprehend,
Or diagnose the beauty,
All is there my willing eyes to take.
To my soul a rosy glow appears,
A gentle warming color to my heart,
A dream, a thought, an image of your face.
These are you, dear Gayle, mysterious hues to blend.
This glow is you, this glow of living light.
I see it now - I can see it now.
* * *

Across my body, a whispering wind appears,
A gentle breath to touch my soul,
To cool my unrestrained passions,
Yet warm to life my latent lusts.
With gentle puffs, as kisses to my mouth,
Bathing me by the wings of wind.
Through my hair the breeze insinuates,
Telling my locks that you are there,

Enveloping my being,
With what I cannot touch,
But only feel.
This is you, dear Gayle, the currents of your sighs.
This wind is you, caressing me with love.
I feel it now - I can feel it now.

* * *

My ears attend to catch the muted sound,
A singing bird, a locust to its mate,
The far off rustling of a million leaves,
Touching hands in welcoming communion,
Impelled by the whisper of the wind,
Vibrations filled with harmony.
They speak of Nature's music.
Silence too rings forth its cadence,
Accenting what is heard,
Transforming noise to song,
And filling the Universe with melody.
Each voice is yours, dear Gayle, the voices of your soul.
An orchestra of love is who you are.
I hear it now - I can hear it now.

* * *

I did not know that life could be so rich,
My dullard mind possessed of self alone,
There were no clues until you happened by,
No hints to open up my empty head.
In ignorance of my soul's deep need,
I was content to wallow in my shallow thoughts,
When you, an open book came by,
To be my teacher strong,
And challenge me to think,
Unbox my stubborn prejudices,
And fertilize my imagination,
Till fresh and unfamiliar plants appeared.
I saw the glow in the sunset clouds,

85

> *I felt the wind from desert corners sent,*
> *I heard the voice from Nature's music box.*
> *Because of you, dear Gayle, because you filled my mind,*
> *An awakening to bliss is who you are.*
> *I know it now - I can know it now.*

There were many special influences on my adult life that challenged me to think about my world. Cundeelee was one of the most significant. Of course there were also my marriages, my children, friendships, study, travel, teaching and more.

Cundeelee made a big impact on my thinking about other cultures – and about myself. Initially the Aborigines did not affect my basic religious perspective very much, but gradually they opened my eyes to the fact that there were other ways of viewing and living in the world that made sense and satisfied their needs – no, more than just satisfied, gave them a view of the world, the cosmos in which they could live as completely as I thought I could in mine.

My Cundeelee experience began in the 1950's when racial prejudices were very stereotyped, and Aborigines were placed at the bottom of the evolutionary scale. We were in the devastating process of undermining the social structures and organizations that had been developed over thousands of years, and destroying significant aspects of their lives. There are still judgmental and prejudiced people around; racists. I think we were among the first to recognize the fantastic qualities of the Aboriginal perspective. I saw boxes other than my own, especially through Toby whom we have met, and later in my Anthropology courses at the University. One thought that impressed me was that Aboriginal religion could not be isolated from all other aspects of their culture. At the university, in our Aboriginal studies, we separated out religion, as we did with social structure, politics, kinship, and economic activities, in order to be able to analyze them, but they were all parts of a complex whole. I was impacted

86

by a new philosophy of life, a new sociological viewpoint, a set of moral and ethical principles and rituals, all of which I barely understood at first, but later took into account in my personal life. The Aborigines respected their environment and took great care of it in both a transcendental manner, and in their practical living.

I was not born Aboriginal, I became one. After 21 years of frequent contact, they ceremonially initiated me into their Aboriginal frame of reference. It was a painful ritual, but that was less significant than the meaning to the Aborigines in accepting me, and the meaning to me of being incorporated into the kinship system and the Aboriginal sacred life. They began the process of the changes in me and were the catalyst for my explorations.

It was at Cundeelee that I began to open my mind, eyes, and ears to the role of language. I realized that my understanding of Aboriginal words and concepts were not the same as that of the Aborigines. So really, in the ideal sense, we were not communicating. My concepts of God and the Devil did not find a place in their mythology, and they were not interpreting my gospel message in the way I thought they should. The word 'blood' was not merely a reference to life blood, or the blood of Christ, but for the Aborigines carried highly sacred, secret and mythological significance that did not correspond to literal blood, and to Christian ideas of sacredness. The core of our message was flawed. I had to think about the implications of that, not only for my understanding of the Aborigines, but for all people everywhere, and also for my perception of myself living in this now arbitrary and linguistically mixed up world. It was my first glimpse into another world, not on its own, but along with other revelations. Lifting the lid of my box I suppose?

I went on to perceive that, like words, each human situation really had no meaning of itself. Each act was a neutral event needing interpretation. I discovered that a single event could

87

be interpreted quite validly in several different ways, one person considering it 'good' while another might say it was 'bad.' Of course this fact was also not new, but in raising my consciousness about it, I began to see it happening all around me. Different definitions of the same situation depended upon a point of view, typically based on the taken for granted assumptions which people used to make their judgments.

I think that the most important point is that we need to live in a Universe that makes sense to us. What we make of it varies from birth onward as we mature and interact with life. It is an absurd world out there, the ultimate chaos. Sadly for some people it drives them mad.

Basic to my thoughts was this challenging conclusion, that because we live in a symbolic universe, giving meaning as we will, there are no Absolutes. Take away the Absolutes and we are freed from the tyranny of the 'Thou shalts' and 'Thou shalt nots'. To be Absolute it must have the qualities of being self-existent, independent, unqualified, unrestricted, and unconditional. It is not relative. I have great difficulty identifying any Absolutes.

If there really *are* Absolutes, what is our responsibility to them, and how do they fit into other aspects of our world view? We would be bound by chains of obedience and inertia, to a stagnant, conservative world view.

If there *are no* Absolutes, what does that mean? Knowing that the Universe is indifferent, we can give our own meaning to it. We have choices from many possibilities. We are liberated from the never changing demands of a never changing Absolute.

If we choose, then we must be responsible for our choices. We cannot blame fate, god's will, other people, luck, our parents, or whatever, for the results of our choices. Taking responsibility for our lives has a great deal of meaning for who we are. We can be Masters of our lives, choosing to the best of our knowledge and ability, or Slaves to others, parents, bosses, church, God/Jesus, or Slaves to our own choices, drugs, tobacco, anger, alcohol, welfare mentality, or any other indulgence that might trap us.

The Master/Slave concept is not necessarily only a political issue, for to some extent we are all 'slaves' to our culture in order to survive socially and economically. However, the 'inner man' can be Master of his own soul, even in the lowliest of circumstances. He may choose, in existential terms, to rise above the poverty of his life. He may be like a sheep, whether led or driven, especially in mass situations (church, sports, fashion, possessions, fads and trends, social class acceptance, etc.). These are not necessarily bad commitments, but it is who you are within them, either mere followers of the mob, or metaphorically standing outside in ecstasy, participating in what the sport, fashion, or religion offers, but not letting them rule you.

Choice and responsibility go together. I faced this matter in my mid-thirties. I had blamed my parents, and many others for some of my life orientations, made them responsible for my faults . . . yes, and my accomplishments. I began to understand that my parents had reared us in difficult times, the Great Depression. My father often beat us and we were never a close knit family.

When I began to take responsibility for my life, I learned to love my father, to understand his childhood experiences, and particularly his mind shattering time in World War I. He had been brutalized throughout his youth, and took it out on my mother and us kids. But he was a hard worker, and provided for us, often at the deprivation of his own needs, and Mum's. He gave me the opportunity to continue at school, something that influenced my life immeasurably. I began to thank him in my mind, and to his face. I stopped being angry and judgmental, and began to love him without conditions. It was a liberating experience. No longer was I trapped under his control, whether he was active in my life or not. Actually there was a reversal of attitude. I began

89

to love him sincerely and unconditionally. I changed my definition of the situation. I also was able to slough off the guilt trip I had imposed on myself and others. I was free at last.

I could no longer make excuses for who or what I am, or what I did. I have noticed that people tend to defend their actions, or explain them in such a way that they themselves do not bear responsibility. "It's not my fault", "Others are to blame". Even small children learn to use these strategies instead of saying, "I did it".

It also dawned on me that people created their own world views to meet their needs in dealing with their environments, and these cosmologies formed the basis for their culture. In that sense, society and culture were not in fact the product of the gods, or the creator beings, but grew out of the demands of the existential realities imposed by nature and human relationships. We invented our gods to satisfy our uncertainties, to give us hope, to give a meaning to tragedy, and to explain the inevitability of death. In short, to provide answers to questions that have no rational answers.

The next leap in my thinking was to recognize that this happened in every society, so that different assumptions led to different cultures and social organizations, and hence to different personalities. The problems I had experienced in working with Aborigines, especially the cultural and religious ones, could now be explained. If I wanted to understand the Aborigines I would need to place my beliefs on one side and open my mind to a different set of propositions about the realities of the universe as seen by the Aborigines. In other words, I needed to take the dirt from my ears and the mud from my eyes.

Perhaps every living thing must make sense of what is there? Animals do it through their instincts and learning, deciding what to eat, mating, migrations, survival. Humans are much the same, but we have demands to make sense beyond mere survival. We have awareness of mental and transcendental possibilities such as humor, play, arts, love, and so on, and of our selves. We are not sure of the nature and extent of animal awareness, but that's another study. For humans it all began with language. Humans began to talk, to create symbolic meaning.

One can become committed to that which has been already established within one's own society through the culture, beliefs, myths, rituals, social/political/personal negotiations, communities, and personal or state territoriality. It is easy to find your pathway, your comfortable boxes, and be content to never move away from them. It takes guts to contemplate changing, and an even greater commitment to make the changes. You change in one element of your life, and that has repercussions in many others. So, even though religion was the most obvious change for me, over time it also led to a re-view of my world, my social world, my belief systems, my behavior.

Particularly following the changes I refer to in this story book, I was able to define my ambitions, to attend to my studies, and to successfully achieve many personal and academic goals. I saw the value in a higher education, and indeed, reveled in the opportunities to teach and to travel.

I have had the privilege of writing stories and poems, many of them tributes to my wife Gayle. She has demonstrated a love for me that transcends mere friendship, and has both engendered and stimulated my creativity.

There is a difference between changing yourself and trying to change others. Both are important, but you need to be aware of the differences. You may change yourself in many ways, but carefully consider whether you have the right to insist on changing others.

I changed, but it was not easy. I had to think carefully every step of the way, meeting the challenge of my own thoughts and decisions, and also taking into account others in my life and outside it. We do affect others. That's why most people remain in their boxes, to please others. Being aware of

91

the effect of your life on others does not mean you must conform to their way of thinking or behaving. You must be true to yourself and follow your own pathway.

Certain parts of their lives are very important to many people, and they try to defend their positions by making judgments, urging you back into their box, or rejecting you from their significant social unit. That was one of the things that made it so difficult to change. They wanted to love me, but it was conditional on my remaining in their "world".

Most of us take our world for granted. We accept what is, because it is comfortable. We live our Truths. But so do others who have their own world views, their own Truths, not only in the larger context of their culture, but sub-culturally, and individually. We define a situation in our terms.

Am I suggesting that you should become a rebel, an odd one out, a deviant? No. Merely that you might follow your own pathway in the fulfillment of your goals. Be very careful what you elect to change. With responsibility, choose positive directions, those which will encourage you to face up to issues rather than run away from them.

DIRT FROM MY EARS, MUD FROM MY EYES

From the Sisyphus milkman tied into routine,
Walking in darkness his soul to redeem,
Accepting the drudgery, with the Book and the Horse,
Fulfilling a purpose, small and simple of course.

A fairytale marriage of learning to share,
All the love we can muster, everywhen, everywhere.
Taking care of our business, with plenty of time,
To step into romance, and find the sublime.

"Despite who would gainsay" the Mckeich family guide,
Challenging the clan to follow with pride
"Go out and do it," whatever that means,

Follow your bliss, wherever that leans.

Take a plane, for your journey, drive or cycle or walk,
And be on your way, don't dawdle or balk,
You may miss the chance, as we did in France,
To visit a village, and join in their dance.

Finding people of interest pursuing their ways,
Quite different from yours, but you'd be amazed,
At the variety of choices that make complete sense,
Once you break down the barriers, and step over the fence.

I did that you know, at remote Cundeelee,
To be respected and honored when they took me,
To become Aboriginal, as best as I could,
To sit down by their fires, and stand where they stood.

I shared in their longing to have back their land,
To them it was more than just bushes and sand.
From there was their life source, a spiritual theme,
Assimilation our war cry, the wickedest scheme.

The death of that old man, from the Dreaming he came,
With respect and with honor they speak not his name.
For a brief passage of time, to this world he was lent,
A proper burial they gave him, and back to the Dreaming
he went.

They opened my vision with a jolt to my mind,
When they told me with confidence, no Absolutes I'd find
I would not believe them, until my thoughts were unbound,
And I puzzled and pondered, but no Absolutes found.

"What did that mean?" I asked in dismay,
And the 'Thou shalts and shalt nots" faded away.
No judgments to make, no putdowns, no hate,

No excuses you offer will sit on your plate.

Take full responsibility for the choices you make,
Be free from the slavery in the directions you take.
Aim for the highest transcendental trails,
Trust in the Universe, and all that entails.

Put away fears,
Achieving the prize,
All the dirt from our ears,
And the mud from our eyes.

This is the life we know. Live it to the fullest of its possibilities for you, so that when you come to the end of your days, as I am, you will be able to say, "I have lived my bliss."

GLOSSARY

Wangkayi – English

(For a more complete reference see: Douglas, W. H., An Introductory Dictionary Of The Western Desert Language, Institute of Applied Language Studies, Western Australian College of Advanced Education, 1988)

inma	ceremony, corroboree
kulila	hear, understand, listen
Kulkopin	place name
kurrti	spirit
miamia	shelter
mirna	cicatrice, scar
Munyurra	Queen Victoria Springs
ngampu yartaka	naked
ngarlturriwa	sorry, sympathetic
ngurrpa	not knowing, uninformed, ignorant
ninti	understand
tjamu	grandfather, grandson
tjilpi	old man
tjitji	child
Tjukurrpa	Dreaming, mythology and philosophy of Aborigines
Tjuntjuntjarra	place name
Walka	red ochre
walypala	whitefella
Wangkayi	people and language of Cundeelee and Warburton
wati	man
yakirri	headband
yuwa	yes

Robert kept and maintained daily personal Journals throughout much of his adult life, in which he recorded his experiences, adventures, observations, insights and wisdom, including his time at Cundeelee. He has donated the Journals and many of the photographs he took over those years to the The State Library of Western Australia (known as the Battye Library). The Journals are available at the library if you would like to know more about Robert or his work, or to use the Journals as a research resource.

http://www.slwa.wa.gov.au/find/wa_information/battye_library

For more information about Robert McKeich and his other books, go to www.robertmckeich.com

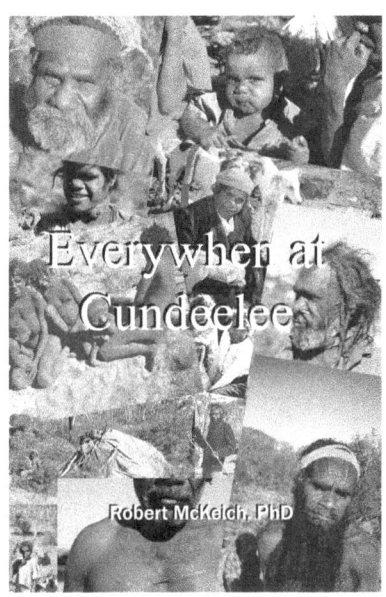

www.ingramcontent.com/pod-product-compliance
Lightning Source LLC
Chambersburg PA
CBHW070203290526
45789CB00002B/897